MEET THE STARS OF
one tree hill

MEET THE STARS OF
one tree hill

by Monica Rizzo

SIMON AND SCHUSTER
London

First published in Great Britain in 2005 by Simon & Schuster UK Ltd.
Africa House, 64-78 Kingsway, London WC2B 6AH
A Viacom Company.

Originally published in the USA in 2005 by Scholastic.

A CIP catalogue record for this book is available from the British Library
upon request.

ISBN 1416904077

1 3 5 7 9 10 6 4 2

Printed and Bound by Cox & Wyman Ltd, Reading, Berkshire.

CONTENTS

INTRODUCTION

Lucas Scott and Nathan Scott live in the same town, go to the same high school, and share a love for basketball. They also have the same father. But that's where their similarities end.

Lucas has been raised by Karen, his single mother, for his entire life. He has never had a relationship with his father, prominent Tree Hill resident Dan Scott, who abandoned Karen when he learned she was pregnant. Karen, meanwhile, has struggled to make ends meet and to teach Lucas to be a solid citizen.

Nathan, on the other hand, has been afforded every want and desire and privilege his father can provide. But it all has a price—and that price is freedom. Dan, a former high school golden boy and star basketball player, wants Nathan to do better than just follow in his footsteps.

While Lucas and Nathan grew up on opposite sides of the tracks, the one thing they do have in common is a desire to discover who they are and who they want to be.

One Tree Hill creator Mark Schwahn originally envisioned a two-hour movie featuring the relationship between two half brothers, the inner workings of a small town, and the central theme of basketball. Mark grew up in an Illinois suburb and learned how family, sports, and small-town politics all affect one another.

"Sports certainly is a metaphor," Mark says of *One Tree Hill*. "Sometimes there are quiet injustices in a small town that sort of hang around for a long time and it makes it harder for kids to find their own way in the face of that. In a lot of families, the parents grew up there and chose to stay, the grandparents grew up there and chose to stay. Sometimes you find that the residue of their actions trickles down to you by default."

The Backstory

Mark's movie script was coming along nicely when he met with producers Brian Robbins and Michael Tollin. Brian and Mike have a successful movie and television production company. When they read Mark's script, they agreed that it would make a nice movie, but an even better television series.

"They said, 'You know, there's so much more here. Instead of spending two hours in this world, why not spend 22 hours in this world every year?'" Mark explains. There was a wealth of material to explore with the characters, their backgrounds, their relationships, their pasts, and their futures. "I said I'd give it a shot and once I wrote the pilot, I was sure they were right."

The show's original title was *An Unkindness of Ravens*. It's a phrase that Lucas explains to Haley in the pilot episode when he tells her that more than one crow is a murder and more than one raven is an unkindness. It's also a reference to the Tree Hill High School basketball team, the Ravens.

Basketball was chosen for several reasons, but mainly because it's one of Mark's favorite sports. A longtime Chicago Bulls fan, Mark knew that a lot of the adversity between Lucas and Nathan could be played out on the basketball court. Small towns tend to rally around their teams. With only five players on each team, it allows for a variety of dramatic one-on-one action.

One thing that didn't work for the network was Mark's title. *An Unkindness of Ravens* was deemed too dark, so Mark decided to shorten it to *Raven*. The new title was a nod to Greek mythology, which speaks of ravens as birds that would guide travelers to their destinations.

"I always felt this was about people who were trying to get someplace, whether it's someplace better or different— they're looking for guidance to get there," Mark says.

But the network still disagreed. They argued that *Raven* had a gothic connotation and that kids wouldn't get it. Then Mark told them that he had named the town Tree Hill after one of his favorite U2 songs, "One Tree Hill."

"I said it's a very personal song," Mark explains, noting that the band wrote the song in memory of one of their crew members who died near One Tree Hill, New Zealand. "I said, really, to me, there's only 'one' Tree Hill, only one place where these kids will grow up, where they will take journeys, where their parents have chosen to reside. This is the 'one' place that is true to all of these characters. It felt really poetic to me."

The network loved it. Thus, a drama was born.

Instant Karma

The studio determined that the pilot would shoot in Wilmington, North Carolina. Mark joined the production crew to scout different locations for the shoot. When it came time to check out the area's gymnasiums, Mark was initially underwhelmed by what he saw. One of the last gyms he looked at was at Laney High School.

"It was a nice gym," Mark says. "But compared to some of the other gyms we'd seen, it didn't have any windows. We love windows because of the natural light."

Mark figured they'd have to keep scouting locations

until someone told him that Chicago Bulls great Michael Jordan went to Laney High School and played basketball in that very gym. In fact, Jordan was cut from the high school basketball team as an underclassman and made the cut the following year thanks to incredible dedication and determination. Jordan has always said that the hurt and humiliation of not making the team was a driving force for him to become the best player he could be—arguably the best player to ever grace the court.

"That's when I said, 'We're done,'" Mark says, laughing. "It was great because from an underdog scenario came the greatest player ever and I thought, 'This is good karma for our show,' because we were very much the underdog from the beginning."

The Underdog Prevails

One Tree Hill was supposed to be a midseason show. It was supposed to go on the air in January 2004. But The WB liked the pilot so much, they decided to put it on the Fall 2003 schedule. That meant a full-out sprint to make the September launch.

When *One Tree Hill* first aired, critics were skeptical. Some reviewers chided the show for having too much teen angst, while others questioned whether they were watching a drama or a basketball game. While ratings dipped, the "little show that could" plodded ahead, fine-tuning plot points and focusing more on the character-rich storylines.

By January 2004, viewers were taking notice. Thanks to a promotional push and savvy programming (The WB reaired episodes of the show on alternate nights), ratings continued to climb. By the season finale in May 2004, The WB had itself a solid hit.

Most of the first season involved introducing and setting up storylines (yes, Haley and Nathan really *did* get married!) to be explored in more detail in season two. Just what lies ahead Mark doesn't want to say.

"I'll be cryptic," Mark says. "I'm an anti-spoiler guy. But I think the audience likes to see Nathan and Lucas as allies. That's a road we'll drive down. I feel like the girls need to have their own journeys. Bethany Joy (Haley) is a wonderful musician and I think there is an arc to be played there with Haley. Peyton is really creative with art and she loves music, so I'd love to see her explore that a bit more as opposed to letting herself be defined by a guy. As for Brooke, we're not so sure she is as happy-go-lucky as she seems. We want to see behind the curtain a bit and really get to know what makes her tick."

As for the adults' storylines, Mark says he is paying close attention to those, too. Will Dan Scott allow Nathan to live his own life, or will he pull him back into the fold? Will he ever reach out to Lucas? Will Karen fall for Keith, or will she allow herself to explore her individuality?

"It's been so rewarding and extremely fulfilling to work with a wonderful crew and cast and tell the stories each week," Mark says. "We make 22 little movies every year and we get to see the audience respond to them. It's a great place to be."

CHAPTER ONE

Chad Michael Murray:
The Beginning

Lucas Scott is an only child being raised by a single mother. A quiet and introspective boy, Lucas learned to deal with being the subject of one of Tree Hill, North Carolina's worst-kept secrets. His biological father, Dan Scott, is one of the town's wealthiest and most prominent citizens. However, Dan chose not to be a part of Lucas's life. Instead, Dan went on to marry another woman. Together they had a son, Nathan, who is just six months younger than Lucas.

For his entire life, Lucas has had to deal with being shunned by townspeople and classmates while Nathan has enjoyed a golden-boy existence, starring on Tree Hill High's basketball team and dating the most beautiful, most popular girl in school.

Sure, Lucas wouldn't mind being popular. But he's skeptical about what it all means. It's understandable that when Lucas is faced with any type of dilemma or obstacle, he proceeds with caution.

The same can be said for Chad Michael Murray, the actor who plays Lucas. Indeed, Chad has never been the type of person who shoots from the hip or responds to key situations with knee-jerk reactions. It's a valuable lesson Chad learned during his boyhood years in Clarence, New York. The small community, which is located near Buffalo, New York, is where Chad was born on August 24, 1981, and where he was raised with his three brothers and one sister.

Because he was part of such a big family, Chad had to learn to speak up if he needed attention. And he did. Sort of. Chad was a happy young kid and he loved to see his family smile, especially when he'd sing and dance. So when he was four and five years old, little Chad fed off of his family's encouragement. After dinnertime, Chad would take center stage in the living room and sing songs he made up about the weather, the trees, trucks—anything his imagination conjured up. He had everyone in stitches with his funny facial expressions and dance moves. Little did Chad know he was building the confidence he'd later need as a professional entertainer. But back then Chad wasn't thinking about what he wanted to be when he grew up. He was just enjoying the good times he had with his family.

The good times, sadly, came to an end when Chad was ten years old. His mother had become very unhappy and decided that she had to leave Buffalo immediately. Her abrupt departure came as a shock to Chad and his siblings. It also put Chad's father, Rex Murray, in a very difficult position of having to work full-time and raise the kids on his own.

Rex worked as an air traffic controller at a local airport. His chosen occupation measures very high on the stress meter. As an ATC, Rex was responsible for making sure that planes had clearance to take off and land. He had to make sure that incoming planes approached the airport from the correct direction and that the landing strip below was clear for their arrival. Oftentimes an ATC communicates with five or six aircraft personnel at one time while simultaneously monitoring computer screens with radar imagery of their flight patterns.

Because the job was so stressful, Rex sometimes just wanted to get home and chill in front of the television. But after Chad's mom left, Rex knew that he had to put the family's needs first. Chad is in awe of his father's commitment to the family. His mother's departure could have ripped the family apart, but instead, Chad says, it made them stronger because it forced them to rely on one another to survive.

"My father is my idol. He's great and I love him," Chad says. "I have no idea how he found strength to raise five kids on his own with a full-time job after losing a marriage of 20 years and being so utterly in love. My father is the strongest man I know and respect.

"He never had time to relax," Chad says of his father's hectic work and family juggling act. "When we were young, he'd get us off to school before he'd go to work as a controller for a nine-hour day, come home, make dinner, make sure we got our homework done, then go right to sleep and do it all over again the next morning."

Chad and his siblings did their part by being good kids. They willingly pitched in with chores around the house, like washing the dishes, running the vacuum cleaner, and keeping their rooms neat. The kids didn't shun their responsibilities because they respected the fact that their dad stood by them and led by example. If work needed to be done around the house, then the Murray clan gladly sacrificed hanging out at the park or going to get ice cream.

Like any ten-year-old, Chad loved to play video games. He was bummed that his dad couldn't give him money to play all the time, but he understood that the family budget was tight. Instead of sulking, Chad took matters into his own hands and got a job delivering newspapers. The paper route gave Chad a lot of responsibility and allowed him to earn his own pocket money. Rex was touched by Chad's ambition.

His dad, Chad says, "is a man who can do everything and doesn't want help from anybody. He can build anything, redo the roof, fix any kind of car, and is a terrific cook. Bless him."

Chad's mother moved back to the Buffalo area when he was a teenager and tried to reconnect with the family. But Chad acknowledges that he and his siblings really don't have much of a relationship with her.

"Unless you've gone through it," Chad explains of being abandoned by a parent, "I don't think you can fully understand what it's like."

As if his mother's abandonment wasn't enough of an ordeal, Chad had yet to experience what he considers were his worst years — his teen years.

It's not easy being a teenager. But for Chad it was even more difficult because he always felt different from the other kids at school. Clarence, New York, is a middle-to-upper-middle-class suburb of Buffalo. Many of Chad's classmates wore the coolest sneakers and jeans to school. But not Chad. Because he was one of five kids in his family, Chad had to wear what his father could afford. Forget wearing designer clothes like Ralph Lauren or Tommy Hilfiger. Ditto for Nike or Adidas sneakers. The family's limited budget meant that hand-me-downs were a given.

"I was a nerd in high school. I was really poor, sort of an outcast," Chad admits. "I wore Payless Shoes and J.C. Penney's clothes, and that will get your (behind) kicked every day in school."

Chad kind of laughs off that kids in school would care what other kids wore. Fashion wasn't what truly mattered to him. Neither were the comments some of the kids would make about his clothes. Chad had a few select friends but basically kept to himself.

"In my own grade, I could count on one hand the people I actually trusted," Chad says. "I didn't like all the peer pressure. The girls didn't want to be with the nerds, so I dated ones from schools 15 or 20 minutes away. They didn't have the misconception of who everyone else thought I was, so they got to know me for me."

When Chad did stay closer to home, he enjoyed reading and studying and hanging out with his older brother Rex's group of friends. Chad was a freshman when Rex was a senior. Yet despite the age gap, Rex's friends were very cool to Chad and made him feel like one of the gang.

"I always hung out with the older kids when I was growing up. I was always about being creative. I like doing things different ways. I never wanted to be trendy or follow the crew. I did my own thing because that's the way my head worked," Chad explains.

After school Chad worked as a janitor at Donut World.

"I got to hang out with cute waitresses and eat donuts for free," Chad says, laughing.

While Chad admits he wasn't into high school, the one thing he did care about was football. It was and still is Chad's number one favorite sport. That's because the city of Buffalo is host to one of the top teams in the NFL — the Buffalo Bills.

Chad and all of his family were big Bills fans. Every Sunday during football season, Chad and his brothers would dress in red and blue, the Bills' team colors. Then they would gather around the television, snacks at arm's length, and watch the game. When the game ended, the boys would talk about the big plays of the day. The guys would often toss the football around and pretend they were throwing a touchdown pass or making a big tackle.

When it came to actually playing the game, Chad was into it 100 percent. He played in the peewee leagues and later was a reserve receiver for the Clarence High Red Devils. He showed up to every practice on time, ran every drill, and became a solid player his teammates could rely on. The team did so well, one year it advanced to the state semifinals.

While Chad wasn't a star player, he did enjoy the game very much. So he was extremely upset when he was injured in a game during his sophomore year. Chad took a hit to the midsection that left him winded and in a lot of pain.

After being taken to the hospital, it was discovered that he had suffered an injury to his small intestine. Chad needed surgery if he was going to live. His father was beside himself as he watched his teenage son wince in pain and discomfort.

The bad news was that Chad required a series of surgeries, which meant a two-month-long hospital stay and an end to playing football. Chad was very upset and disappointed when he heard the news. He knew that he would probably never play college or pro ball. Football was the one sport he really loved to play. And now he couldn't.

During his stay at the hospital, Chad got to know many of the medical staff. One day one of the nurses who was treating Chad offered him some encouraging advice. She convinced him that there was more to life than football. In fact, she convinced him that he might have what it took to build a successful career as a model. After all, he was tall and thin and very good-looking.

"She was a model on the side and thought I should be a model, too," Chad says, noting that he told her he didn't want to be a model but had wondered what it would be like to be an actor.

"She convinced me that I could segue from modeling into acting. I finally saw the light," Chad says.

CHAPTER TWO

Chad: *Model Citizen*

Looking Good

Chad took that nurse's advice to heart. He loved watching movies that starred his favorite actors, Robert DeNiro and Al Pacino. He looked at actor Edward Norton and thought, *I wonder if I could do that?* Ed was a tall, skinny kid who blossomed into a critically acclaimed actor. Chad looked at Ed as a role model of sorts. The more he thought about it, the more Chad knew he had what it took to become an actor, even if it meant becoming a model first.

A visit to Buffalo's Wright Models validated Chad's beliefs. He was promptly signed and enlisted to do some local modeling work for catalogs and newspaper ads. Chad pursued his newfound career while finishing up his studies at Clarence High. Soon after graduating in June 1999, Chad trekked to a modeling convention in Orlando, Florida.

Orlando was quite a culture shock for Chad. Not only was the city jammed with tourists heading to Disney

World, but it featured palm trees, sunny skies, and tons of beautiful people. Orlando is known as a proving ground of sorts for many aspiring performers. Musical groups like the Backstreet Boys, *NSYNC, and LFO got their start in Orlando.

Chad soaked up the scene at the Orlando Convention Center, where he was surrounded by hundreds of aspiring or working models. It was there that Chad met an agent by the name of Eddie Winkler. Eddie was a veteran at spotting budding talent. When he met Chad, he knew right away that there was only one place for him—Los Angeles. Even though New York is generally regarded as the modeling capital, Eddie knew that Chad's lanky six-foot frame, blond spiky hair, and blue eyes would be a hit with the L.A. modeling agencies. New York male models tend to have darker, brooding looks. Chad could do brooding, but he also had the right kind of smoldering-yet-optimistic looks that are more sought after with West Coast agencies.

Eddie offered to pay for Chad's expenses if Chad, in turn, would agree to travel to Los Angeles to meet another agent named Bonnie Liedtke. The trip was supposed to only be for seven days. But when Bonnie met Chad, she knew she could get him work in no time. And she did. Within weeks Chad was going out on jobs for local department store ads. And it wasn't long before he caught the attention of campaign managers for fashion heavyweights like Skechers, Tommy Hilfiger, and Gucci.

"I started modeling pretty fast," Chad says, still bewildered at his launch into show business. "I never wanted to model. It isn't something that I'm interested in. It is just what I needed to pay the bills. I don't find it creative and I don't enjoy it."

In a word, Chad found the work to be boring. He felt odd being paid to stand still and look handsome. Then again, the modeling afforded him a one-bedroom apartment, new clothes, and the opportunity to meet people in the acting world. Thanks to Bonnie, Chad met a talent manager and acting coach named John Simmonds. John gave Chad the help he needed to learn the craft of acting.

After working with John for several months, Chad went on several acting auditions. The first one to come through was a guest-starring role on the PAX TV series *Chicken Soup for the Soul*. In his episode Chad played a rich kid who didn't like his family. The fledgling cable show didn't have a very large audience, but Chad was thrilled nonetheless. After all, this was his big breakthrough into the acting world. He was pumped and couldn't wait until it was time to audition for his next role.

The WB network is known for taking unknown actors and turning them into major stars. That was true for every one of the teen actors on *Dawson's Creek*, not to mention most of the actors on *Buffy the Vampire Slayer*, *Roswell*, and *7th Heaven*. In early 2000, Chad heard that The WB was casting for a show called *Day One*. He showed up to the audition in Burbank, California, to find 50 people waiting for him. The room was full of network executives, casting directors, and producers. Chad was nervous, but he took a deep breath and then read through his lines. After he finished, Chad was thanked for his time, and then called aside by one of the network executives. He asked Chad if they could set up a meeting as soon as possible.

The show *Day One* never did end up being made. But The WB honchos liked what they saw in Chad. At the meeting, Chad was offered a development deal with the network. Basically, The WB felt Chad was a strong enough talent that they wanted to make sure he stayed within the Warner Brothers family. The deal was great for Chad, too, because he had the network's commitment that they were going to try to find roles and projects that would challenge and fulfill him as an actor.

Later that same year, a little show called *Gilmore Girls* premiered on The WB. The show—about single mom Lorelai Gilmore and her teenage daughter, Rory—received rave reviews from television critics across the country. Rory, played by actress Alexis Bledel, was a model student who had looks, brains, and a cute boyfriend. It was all so, well, nice. Nice, that is, until Tristan DuGrey showed up.

That's the character Chad was tapped to play during the show's premiere season. A smart-aleck, blue-blood prep school teen, Tristan took an interest in Rory and rocked her world.

Tristan, Chad says, is the kind of rich kid who got everything he ever wanted. "The way he sees Rory is: 'Well, what the heck is going on here? Why isn't she falling for me?' I think he took it personally," Chad says.

Tristan tried to get Rory's attention, but she rebuffed his advances. Chad found the role a delight to play because it was so different from the kind of high school experience he had. Plus, it was a lot of fun to get to know the *Gilmore Girls* cast. Chad and Alexis hit it off instantly because they both were at the beginning of their respective acting careers. Alexis had modeled a bit while growing up in Houston, which also struck a common chord with Chad.

Actor Jared Padalecki, who played Rory's boyfriend Dean, became a close pal of Chad's, too. In fact, the guys got along so well, it was sometimes difficult for them to do their work. The two spent a lot of time goofing around, making jokes, and pretend-fighting with each other.

"When we did the fight scene in one of the episodes, it was a lot of fun because we got to scream at each other," Chad explains. "We weren't really worried that we were gonna hit each other. But sure enough, Jared was getting pulled back by the guys and he was swinging his arms.

And they let go of his arm and it popped me right in the mouth. I had a big ol' fat lip for the rest of the day."

That same year Chad also landed a guest-starring role on the show *Diagnosis Murder*. He played a teenage boy who had an affair with an older woman, murdered her husband, and got caught.

With these two roles under his belt, in 2001 Chad was quickly signed up for a recurring role on the already established WB hit show *Dawson's Creek*. This time Chad played college boy Charlie Todd, a bass guitarist who enters a relationship with Jen Lindley (actress Michelle Williams). Charlie was basically a nice guy, but somewhat of a player when it came to the ladies.

The experience was a lot of fun for Chad because he made some good friends and became acquainted with the town of Wilmington, North Carolina, where *Dawson's* was filmed. Chad and actor Kerr Smith hung out from time to time, grabbed a bite to eat at the Slice of Life pizzeria, or downed coffee at the local coffeehouse. It was a pivotal time for Chad, whose work on *Dawson's* gained him a lot of attention from Hollywood producers. Chad also landed a role in the TV movie *Aftermath*, which starred well-known actors Robert Urich and Meredith Baxter.

In 2002 Chad won a guest spot on *CSI: Crime Scene Investigation* and filmed the made-for-TV movie *The Lone Ranger*, which aired on The WB in 2003. Chad played the lead character Luke Hartman. The movie focused on the Lone Ranger's early years, much like how the television show *Smallville* focuses on Superman's early years. The film received lukewarm reviews from the critics. But one thing the critics couldn't deny was Chad's appeal. He was being hailed as the next big thing in Hollywood. And the critics were right.

A much-talked-about remake of the 1976 film *Freaky Friday* was going to shoot in the Los Angeles area. The movie is about a mother and daughter who trade identities for a day and live out each other's lives. Jamie Lee Curtis was tapped to play mom Tess Coleman and hot rising star Lindsay Lohan signed on to play her daughter, Anna Coleman. Chad was cast as high school boy Jake, Anna's love interest. While his wasn't a lead role, Chad was thrilled at the chance to play opposite these two talented actresses.

"Jake's a normal high school guy. He's the tween version of a bad boy. He rides a Ducati motorcycle and wears a leather jacket. So, of course, as a mother he's the guy you don't want your daughter dating," Chad says. "But he's also incredibly intelligent and he likes Anna's music. He's really genuine. He's a gentleman. But the surface doesn't really show that.

"He basically goes after Anna, and when Anna and Tess switch bodies, he ends up following Anna's personality into the mother's body and becomes fixated on her. He ends up flirting with both the girls. Man, I got confused, but I got a kick out of it," Chad says, laughing.

Like Chad, Lindsay was one of Hollywood's most celebrated young talents. Everybody was buzzing about how she was going to be "the next big thing." And Jamie Lee Curtis? The veteran actress has proved in her career that she can handle dramatic roles just as easily as comedic roles. Luckily for everyone, this was a comedy. Indeed, Chad found himself in situations that could have been awkward had he not been able to deflect them with his great sense of humor.

Most people remembered Lindsay's star turn in the 1998 remake of *The Parent Trap*. Lindsay was 12 at the time that movie came out. She was short, with red hair and a freckled face. So when *Freaky Friday* came out, everyone was in awe of how much she had grown into a beautiful, mature-looking 16-year-old.

Even though Lindsay and Chad had a six-year age difference, the two got along like gangbusters. They had fun on the set, especially when Jamie Lee bought a Ping-Pong table for everyone to play with while they were shooting the movie. But more important than just getting along, Chad and Lindsay shared a very special bond.

Lindsay explains that she had her first-ever on-screen kiss in *Freaky Friday* with Chad. She admits she was nervous about it, but Chad was ever the gentleman. Must have been all the practice he got while filming *Gilmore Girls* and *Dawson's Creek.*

Freaky Friday was a big success for Disney but an even bigger success for Chad. It proved that he could portray a strong, charismatic presence on the big screen. It also proved that he could take on anything.

Still, the best was yet to come for Chad.

CHAPTER THREE

Chad: *One Tree Hill Climber*

Every January through March, new television shows called pilots are written, cast, and filmed for the networks to see. Dozens of shows are filmed in hopes of having a network commit to putting it on the air that following September or, in some cases, in January, the middle of the television season.

In early 2003, Chad was asked to look over several scripts for pilots that were shooting for the upcoming television season. Like a lot of actors, Chad had been down this road many times before. But this time around, because he was becoming a more established young star on the Hollywood scene, Chad had a plethora of projects to peruse. A couple of the projects were generating a steady buzz around industry circles. One was a drama called *The O.C.* about Orange County, California, teenagers and their families. The other show, *One Tree Hill*, also centered around teenagers, their family dynamics, basketball, and some secrets in a small North Carolina beach town.

Having just come off very successful back-to-back guest-starring stints on *Gilmore Girls* and *Dawson's Creek*, Chad knew that his next role had to be a good one. Given that he was reading for the lead role for each show, Chad weighed his decision carefully. He liked the role of Ryan Atwood on *The O.C.* because the character had a lot of depth. Ryan was abandoned by his father and later his mother. He didn't come from money, but he knew right from wrong. All Ryan needed was a chance to prove he could succeed, and he got that when a sympathetic Orange County attorney brought him home to live with his family.

Chad's other consideration was the role of Lucas Scott on *One Tree Hill*. Lucas, an only child, was abandoned by his father before he was born. As he grew up, he learned that his father, Dan Scott, was actually one of Tree Hill's most prominent citizens. Soon after Dan left Lucas's mom, he got another woman pregnant. They married and had a son, Nathan. Lucas and Nathan, students at the same high school, were worlds apart. Popular Nathan is Tree Hill High's top basketball star. He comes from money, drives a hot new Mustang, and can date any girl he wants. Lucas, meanwhile, is introverted, prefers reading to socializing, and is lucky if girls will acknowledge him, let alone go out with him.

When Chad really put his mind to it, it wasn't too difficult to make the decision to go for *One Tree Hill*. The subject matter really hit home for Chad. He and Lucas had a lot in common. Chad didn't come from money. He never felt like he fit in while he was in high school. Like Lucas, Chad was raised by a single parent. As an actor, Chad felt like he hit the jackpot when he read this role because he knew that he could translate his own real-life experience into this character.

"As an actor, it gives me a distinct advantage because I feel like I've got a great opportunity to make it real, to connect with people because it happened to me," Chad explains.

When Chad read for the *One Tree Hill* production team, they instantly knew he was perfect for the role. He felt the same way, too, except for one thing—the relationship Lucas has with his mother, Karen.

"I was nervous at first about building a relationship with the mother," Chad says. "I never had one, so I didn't know what I should do. I kind of played off my father."

Chad discussed his feelings with Moira Kelly, the actress who plays Lucas's mother. Through Lucas, Chad is able to look to Moira for something he would have loved to have had when he was growing up. Since *One Tree Hill* started filming, Chad says he's grown more and more comfortable portraying Lucas.

"I use my work as therapy to look from the outside in. It's nice to take a character and get him to rise above the negativity around him," Chad says.

Rising above negativity proved to be a challenge for Chad and his fellow *One Tree Hill* costars. When the show premiered on September 23, 2003, it was not embraced by television critics. What's worse, in the weeks that followed, viewers just weren't tuning in. The *One Tree Hill* gang wondered what their fate would be. Would the show be able to hang in there? Would the network want to cut its losses and pull the plug? Or would they try to make it work? Everyone poured their hearts and souls into the show, and what's more, they had left their lives behind to move to Wilmington, North Carolina. Nobody wanted it to end, but reality was looking pretty bleak.

"Everyone was really panicky when the first ratings came out," Chad said. "Everyone was just freaking out. I was the only person that laughed. I laughed absolutely hysterically. I thought it was great! Man, if we're going to suck, dude, I want to be at the bottom of the barrel so we can climb up."

There might have been a moment that Chad wondered "what if?" After all, had he chosen the role of Ryan on *The O.C.* he would be on a show that was both critically acclaimed and an instant fan favorite. But of course, wondering about what might have been isn't Chad's style.

Actor Benjamin McKenzie owned the role of Ryan, just as Chad made his mark with Lucas. Chad knew that he had made the right decision. Like he had done all his life, he hung in there.

"As cheesy as it might sound, I always called us 'The Little Show That Could,'" Chad says. "We aren't big or flashy or high-concept, but we have a lot of heart."

Meanwhile, the show made some creative changes. Chad and *OTH* costar James Lafferty were putting in mega hours rehearsing for the show's basketball scenes. TV critics suggested that perhaps the show should focus more on the interpersonal dynamics of the friends and families and not so much on the basketball. *OTH* producers agreed and gradually made the hoops connection a little less prominent. The adjustment not only saved the production time and money, it also enabled Chad and James to focus more on their characters instead of lengthy choreographed court scenes.

With a little more free time to spend with the scripts, Chad was able to really sink his teeth into the show's material. His performances shone a little brighter, as did those of his fellow cast members. And people—critics and viewers—took notice.

By January 2004, the show had finally found its groove. Even better news, the show had found its audience. *One*

Tree Hill rose steadily in the ratings to become one of the top five television shows among teenage girls.

It wasn't long after that The WB decided to renew *OTH* for a second season. Chad and the gang were ecstatic. They knew the show was a winner. What's more, they loved working together. They all had become great friends. And in Chad's case, he had developed a very close bond with costar Sophia Bush.

The two connected as friends from the moment they shot the pilot. Their friendship blossomed into a quiet romance during the first half of the first season. Chad and Sophia enjoyed long talks over dinner and walks along the beach.

It wasn't unusual for Chad and Sophia to spend time together since their characters, Lucas and Brooke, were dating. Many of the *OTH* crowd just assumed that when Chad and Sophia were together they were rehearsing scenes or talking about the show or just plain hanging out like coworkers often do. Little did they know the two actors had a secret.

In Hollywood, it's not at all uncommon for actors to meet on a project and begin dating. What is uncommon is for the relationship to last. Many times actors fall for each other while they're working and enjoy a whirlwind romance. Then, as time goes on, they discover that maybe they didn't have so much in common. It can be an awkward situation at best.

"I've had multiple on-screen relationships that never made me want to date any of those people," Chad explains. But Sophia, he says, was different.

"It's not like there was an attraction based solely on work. We click well," Chad says.

Chad and Sophia were aware of the pitfalls of dating a coworker. They decided to proceed slowly and keep their budding social life under wraps. There were no outward signs of their union — no gazing into each other's eyes, no public displays of affection. On the set, it was business as usual.

But the more time they spent together, the more they knew their attraction to each other was real. Only one thing troubled them — how would they tell their cast mates?

"We kept it from everybody for about a month because we didn't know exactly how everyone was going to react," Chad explains. "And we wanted to be sure that we were going to be serious as a couple. But when we knew this was real, we got sick of keeping it from everyone."

Rather than make a big production about things, Chad had an idea. He decided that he and Sophia should just go about their business and let people discover on their own. One night the cast decided to get together for dinner in downtown Wilmington. Everybody was seated at a big table. Dinner was on the table and conversation was flowing when Chad decided to plant a sweet-yet-passionate kiss right on Sophia's lips.

"Everyone was sitting around us, calmly going, 'Hey, that's great. So when did this happen?'" Chad says, laughing.

By season's end, Chad and Sophia's romance was old news. What was a bigger deal for them was heading to Australia, where Chad would film the movie *House of Wax*. Because Chad was starring in the movie, the two knew they wouldn't have a ton of time together. Still, both of them were excited to explore the land down under. Neither of them had ever been to Australia, so it was a chance to see a new country, meet some new people, and be together away from the prying eyes of reporters and photographers.

Sad but true, Chad and Sophia had become gossip-column fodder when they decided to hook up. Thankfully neither of them had yet to experience any run-ins with rude journalists or paparazzi. But still, given that their relationship was still young, both were thankful to be going to a place where nobody really knows their name. At least, not yet.

CHAPTER FOUR

Chad: *Man with a Vision*

In the summer of 2004, Chad was hard at work in Australia filming *House of Wax*. The movie is about teens who encounter some car trouble. They make their way to a gas station only to find that its owner is a sick, demented human being. The owner then torments the teens, a captive audience of sorts as they are stranded without their wheels. Other stars in the movie include Chad's buddy *Gilmore Girls* star Jared Padalecki; *The Simple Life*'s Paris Hilton; and *24*'s Elisha Cuthbert.

While filming, Chad had to take a break and travel back to the United States—Los Angeles, to be exact—to promote the movie he shot in the summer of 2003, *A Cinderella Story*. The 15-hour flight was worth it, though, as Chad celebrated his first leading film role opposite teen queen and close pal Hilary Duff.

The movie is a modernization of the classic fairy tale. Hilary, natch, is the "Cinderella" in the movie, only her character's name is actually Sam Montgomery. Her Prince Charming—Chad—is fellow classmate and resident high school jock Austin Ames. Sam—an introverted teenager who lives with her self-involved stepmother, Fiona (actress Jennifer Coolidge), and her two not-so-nice stepsisters—meets Austin in an online chat room.

Both Austin and Sam seem to bask in the anonymity of online chatting rather than revealing themselves to each other. This aspect of the film, teamed with the irony of playing a character whose high school existence was completely opposite his own, appealed to Chad.

"I was Sam in high school, Sam the nerd—that was me," Chad says. "I had no friends, I used to walk through the halls at school worried about getting slammed into a locker. That's why it's funny for me to be walking down those hallways again—like high school all over again, except that now I get to be the cool guy."

Outwardly, Austin seems to have it all. He's totally hot, he's popular, he drives a cool car, he's the captain of the football team, and he could probably date any girl he wants. Behind the facade, Austin yearns for something more. Portraying that kind of conflict was appealing to Chad.

"It was a great opportunity to fake the stereotypical jock thing, to play that and yet have an underlying sensitivity and conflict," Chad explains. "There's always a sadness to Austin. He's so busy being the guy his parents want him to be or his friends want him to be that he can't take a break to figure out what he wants to be."

Getting to know Hilary was a blast for Chad. Despite the difference in their ages, the two actors got along like gangbusters—almost by design. Chad and Hilary knew that they were playing each other's love interest in the film. What they didn't know was that their first on-screen kiss was going to happen just days into shooting. They'd barely gotten past the "Good morning, how ya doin?" stage before they were directed to lip-lock under Hollywood-style rainy skies.

"We barely knew each other," Chad says, laughing, noting that there were dozens of the film's production crew watching the scene be filmed. "It was a big scene and it had to be raining, so we were being pelted with these big fat drops of fake rain, because regular-sized rain doesn't show up well on camera. I'm talking quarter-sized drops of water dropping down on us. Imagine a waterfall going over your face and every time you try to breathe while you're kissing, bubbles go up in your nose or water goes into your mouth. Fun, right?"

Chad jokes about the memorable scene that left him and Hilary in stitches. Needless to say, they became close friends after that close encounter. All kidding aside, Chad says the scene definitely makes for a wonderful moment in the film.

"It was really sweet, a great scene. And I know that when people watch it they're not going to care what may have been going on around us," Chad says.

Chad filmed *A Cinderella Story* in Los Angeles in the summer of 2003, and wrapped the film literally days before he had to fly to Wilmington to start work on *One Tree Hill*. He barely had time to think about how exciting it was to have his first major feature film role in the bag and a starring role on a major television drama. Then again, Chad isn't one to rest on his laurels. He's constantly thinking of ways to challenge himself as an actor.

One of Chad's idols in the acting world is Edward Norton. Ed burst onto the Hollywood scene in the 1996 film *Primal Fear*. His performance earned him an Oscar nomination. Since then, Ed has been regarded as one of Hollywood's most versatile talents.

Ed's career is one Chad would like to model his own after. And Chad wouldn't mind starring alongside Ed someday, too.

"I think the greatest validation would be, at the end of the day, him patting me on the shoulder and going, 'Wow, kid—you held your own. I gotta study my lines a little better tomorrow,'" Chad says, laughing. "That's a goal to shoot for."

And it's a goal he might well achieve. In 2004 Chad was named one of *Teen People*'s Hot 25 Under 25. He also found himself on *Entertainment Weekly*'s It List. Industry insiders covet lists like these because they highlight entertainment's hottest stars. Chad is flattered by the accolades but doesn't hold too much stock in them. After all, for Chad it's all about building a career, not being the flavor of the month.

Homeboy

As often as he can, Chad likes to visit his family in Buffalo. Sometimes, if the show is on a long enough hiatus, Chad hops in the car and drives up the coast to Buffalo. When time is less abundant, Chad will hop on a plane.

When he's home, Chad enjoys talking with his brothers and sister about what they're up to. Meantime, all they want to know is what his life is like. Sure, Chad is excited about what he does, but he doesn't let the fame and money go to his head—though sometimes his fame is hard to escape. Chad's younger sister, Shannon, thinks her big brother is awesome. And so do her friends.

"My little sister's friends are like, 'He's cute,' and all that," Chad says, laughing.

Even though he might get teased from time to time, Chad knows his family is behind him 100 percent. They always have been. Never once did anyone, especially his father, Rex, discourage him from pursuing his dream to become an actor.

"He had a lot of faith," Chad says of his father. "He knew it was going to happen and it was going to work. He is completely there for me."

Chad has a soft spot for his hometown. In addition to seeing his family, he misses the small-town feel of the city. "I loved Buffalo. So many people take it for granted. Take the peacefulness of it. It is such a safe and a good environment," Chad says.

The first time Chad got homesick for Buffalo was when he was standing in line at a Burger King restaurant in Los Angeles. New to the city, 18-year-old Chad just wanted to stop and grab a bite to eat at an affordable and familiar place. Next thing he knew, three guys had jumped him.

"I had my nose put on the other side of my face," Chad recalls. "It was three guys. What the hell was I supposed to do? The doctors didn't even bother running X-rays. They just reset it. But it wasn't a nose job."

In fact, the nose incident turned out to be Chad's big break, so to speak. People told Chad that he was "too pretty" to be an actor. When his nose healed, it took on a slightly different form, thus giving him perhaps an edgier look.

But that was then and this is now. Chad is still sitting pretty, nose and all. His treks back to Buffalo are now heralded by the masses. The people who once mistreated him and made fun of him when he was a kid now greet him with smiles and handshakes. They want to talk to him and buy him a drink. Chad shrugs off the star treatment because he knows that deep down inside he's the same person now that he was then. The sucking up he experiences is only mildly appealing to him in the sense that he has a degree of satisfaction that he is having a successful career and living a happy life.

"If my happiness rubs it in their face, then fine. But it's not about that. I enjoy what I do and that's what it is all about," Chad says.

Downtime

When Chad isn't working, he enjoys spending time at his homes in Wilmington or Los Angeles reading or watching old movies. For fun he collects autographed sports memorabilia and keeps his closet stocked with new Nike sneakers and football jerseys.

While he does like to keep busy, Chad also enjoys zoning out every now and again. During the pro-football season, don't bother Chad. Every Sunday he can be found front and center on the couch watching football. Just like he did when he was a kid, Chad puts on a blue-and-red

Buffalo Bills jersey and watches game after game after game. Game day is the one day he's content with doing absolutely nothing.

Chad also enjoys quiet times with Sophia. When they are shooting the show, the couple enjoys dining in one of Wilmington's cozy restaurants. They also enjoy long conversations about life and literature. Chad can't help but gush when he talks about why he became smitten with Sophia.

"She's very intelligent and she reads every night. She's into art and photographs," Chad says, noting that Sophia is quite the classy young lady. "She's not promiscuous. She's not at all like her character."

What's true of Chad—both in real life and on TV—is that he's a great listener with a very generous heart. One time the two of them were talking and Sophia revealed that her favorite car was a 1965 Mustang. It's probably one of America's all-time classic car models. Chad matter-of-factly acknowledged to Sophia that the '65 Mustang was a cool set of wheels. Secretly, though, the wheels in his head began to turn. When she wasn't around, Chad fervently searched for one that he could buy. He found it, had it restored to its original condition, and presented it to his beloved as a gift.

"It's our family car," Chad jokes.

Chad is also very much aware of how his celebrity status affects teens who look up to him as a role model. That's why he lives a clean, healthy lifestyle. At least three days a week, Chad can be found working out at the gym, lifting weights and running on the treadmill. He shuns cigarettes and alcohol because he knows they don't do anything to help a person, only hurt them.

"I want to get to a point in my career where I can be a role model. A good one," Chad says. "I want to say 'I got here without drugs and I got here without drinking or smoking. If I can do it, you can do it. I have no doubt.' I really want kids to have a chance in life."

CHAPTER FIVE

James Lafferty Is Nathan Scott

Nathan Scott appears to have it all. As the star of the Tree Hill Ravens basketball team, Nathan is one of the most popular kids in town. He's good-looking, comes from a wealthy family, and gets just about whatever he wants. Or does he? Viewers saw behind the facade in *One Tree Hill*'s first season and discovered that Nathan is an unhappy young man who's tired of living his father's dream. His father, Dan Scott, wants Nathan to live the life he himself didn't get to experience. He wants Nathan to be a star and his pursuit of that goal drove a wedge through their relationship.

Nathan's father always told him that he should steer clear of his half brother, Lucas. But Nathan slowly realizes that he might have an ally in Lucas. As Nathan reevaluates his life, he's learning that maybe there is more in this world than basketball.

Actor James Lafferty is an avid basketball fan and was immediately interested in portraying Nathan.

"It was a television show and yeah, it was about basketball, but it was really character-driven. I knew Mark Schwahn's writing from *The Perfect Score*, so I knew I was going into it with good people," James says.

James was born on July 25, 1985, in Hemet, California, to Angie and Jeff Lafferty, who own a local construction business. Hemet is a rural town located approximately 90 miles east of Hollywood. It's a quiet place known for its spectacular lake and proximity to the popular desert resort town of Palm Springs.

The small-town community was a great place to grow up for James and his younger brother, Stuart. The boys enjoyed swimming, hiking, and sports like basketball and football.

"It was very nice," James says fondly of Hemet. "I was able to have a really great childhood growing up because it was a small town. I had the same friends all the way through high school."

When James and Stuart were in elementary school, they discovered acting through a friend of their mother's. The friend's daughters had gotten some work in different television and movie projects. It sounded like fun so Angie mentioned it to James and Stuart one night at dinner. The idea was met with great enthusiasm and Angie immediately started investigating what it would take for her boys to enter the entertainment business.

Turns out it took the right blend of looks and talent. Angie willingly drove the hour-and-a-half route every time the boys were called into Los Angeles or, more often, Burbank to audition for roles. The commuting soon paid off when seven-year-old James landed some work as an extra on the television show *Picket Fences* and in the movie *Batman Returns*.

"When we got a little older she asked us if we wanted to take it a little more seriously and we said we wanted to. So we dedicated ourselves to it a little bit more," James says.

The dedication meant taking professional acting classes and being ready at a moment's notice to show up at a casting director's office and audition. James and Stuart both were up to the task.

As much as James pursued acting outside of school, inside the halls of Hemet High School he had a different passion — basketball. James was one of the star players of the Hemet Bulldogs team. He didn't get involved with the drama club at school, he says, because he wanted to keep his professional aspirations and his personal aspirations separate.

"I did plenty of auditioning and acting classes in L.A. and I didn't really bring it to school. If I ever got a job, I'd have to leave school for a while and the teachers were really supportive. I never had to leave for too long."

In the fall of 2001, James got his first big role when he landed the part of Emeril Lagasse's son on the NBC sitcom *Emeril*. The famous chef had developed quite a following with his cable cooking show. People not only tuned in to see his culinary creations, they enjoyed his over-the-top comedic personality. The network thought Emeril might be able to cross over to the mainstream in a traditional sitcom world. The idea came from a tried-and-true formula. For years, stand-up comedians have launched sitcoms based on their personal lives. NBC thought it would be great to have Emeril star as himself—a television personality who also has a wife and family. It's very similar to when Tim Allen starred in the hit ABC comedy *Home Improvement*.

James was tapped to play Emeril's son in the show. Even though the show didn't last more than several episodes, it was a high-profile project that attracted a lot of media attention and gave James a lot of exposure.

"That was probably the biggest thing I'd done at that time," James says. "I did a lot of publicity for it and I got a lot of experience," James says.

James wasn't too young to be considered for the lead role in the 2002 TV movie *A Season on the Brink*. The movie is based on author John Feinstein's bestselling book about a year in the life of the Indiana Hoosiers basketball team at Indiana University. IU has a rich basketball tradition and regularly attracts some of the nation's top high school players to its program. The book focused on one particular season—1985–86—and one particular player at IU—a young man by the name of Steve Alford. Steve was a top college player and was believed to be the key to IU's success.

Because James was a solid actor and an exceptional basketball player, he was called in to read for the part.

"It was really exciting, actually," James says. "I'm a big basketball fan. I've been playing all my life. It was definitely a dream role. Going into the audition I didn't know who Steve Alford was. He was playing at Indiana when I was born. But I watched a lot of games on tape and he's got this perfect jump shot. I got the book and read it on the plane ride on the way to do the movie."

Looking back, James says he's not sure which aspect of the movie appealed to him the most. "I got as much into the basketball part of it as I did into the acting part of it and it became a really, really memorable experience for me," he explains. "It's funny because I was so young—I was only 16—and I was playing a college basketball player in a big movie. I came back from that experience a better basketball player and a better actor."

During his senior year of high school, James had set his sights on college. He worked hard at getting good grades and playing the best basketball he could. The Bulldogs had a solid team for the 2002–2003 season, and James was a big part of the reason. His signature 15-foot jump shots helped the team win many games and earned him the MVP award that year.

James decided he would attend California State University at Long Beach. The school was close enough to home if he wanted to visit his family on weekends, but far enough away that he could have a life to himself. Things seemed to be in place in the spring of 2003 when James was called to audition for *One Tree Hill*. The producers were familiar with his work from *A Season on the Brink* and wanted to see if he'd be interested in reading for another basketball player role.

"I was all set to go to college, get a dorm room, go to orientation, and all that," James explains. "I had the audition for *One Tree Hill* and I booked it, so I had to put college on hold."

James couldn't believe that he could be so lucky to get another shot at playing a guy who loves basketball. But there was more to Nathan Scott than just hoops.

"It was a challenging role to play because it had a lot of levels," James says.

Drawing upon one's personal experiences is a technique many actors employ when stepping into a role. James says that was definitely true when he took on Nathan Scott.

"I think no matter what character you play, there's always something in there you can relate to on some level. Even though I didn't have any experiences with my family like Nathan did, I'm able to draw on his competitive drive and his drive to be the best and make the best for himself," James says. "He's got a conscience. He knows the difference between right and wrong, just like everybody else, and he struggles with it, just like everybody else."

Another thing James has in common with Nathan is adjusting to being on his own. About a month after James graduated from high school, he had to move to Wilmington to work on the show. On one hand, working on a television series was exciting to James. But on the other hand, he knew he was going to miss his family very much.

Because of Wilmington's easygoing way of life, James often feels like he's still living in a small town. He enjoys exploring the sights on weekends and eating out.

"There's a ton of restaurants in Wilmington," James says. "I go out all the time. I have a few places I really like to go, so I rotate a lot."

Just because his mother isn't around doesn't mean

James slacks off when it comes to chores. Most days off are spent playing basketball, working out, and running errands.

"I have to get all that stuff done that I can't do during the week—clean up, do my laundry," James says, noting emphatically, "I don't have a maid."

What the future holds for James is up in the air. Some days he thinks he might want to still try to go to college, and other days he thinks he might want to continue with acting.

"It really depends on how old I am and where my career is going by then," says James.

Indeed, acting isn't what's foremost on James's mind 24/7. While most actors thrive on getting as many projects going as they can, James made a decision to take the summer following the first season of *One Tree Hill* off.

"We really work a lot when we're down in North Carolina. We don't get a whole heck of a lot of time to smell the roses, so I kind of reaped the benefits of all the good fortune I've had the first year and just kind of hang out with my friends back home, playing basketball and trying to stay in shape."

Because of *OTH*'s popularity, James has found himself the center of attention wherever he goes. He finds his teen idol status a bit odd at times.

"It's definitely a different experience for me and something I'll probably never get used to," says James, who doesn't buy into being a teen magazine hottie.

Most of his fans are female and most of them do tell him they think he's cute. They are excited to meet him and usually ask him for an autograph and maybe a picture. While he's extremely flattered, James says he doesn't pay any mind to all of the attention.

"It's all part of the ride, I guess," James says. "We have really great fans, really dedicated fans, people who really enjoy our show and we're really appreciative of that."

CHAPTER SIX

Hilarie Burton Is Peyton Sawyer

Take one look at Peyton Sawyer and she appears to have it all going on and then some. Medusalike curls frame the beautiful face of Tree Hill High's most popular cheerleader. She wears her school colors proudly and puts on a good show for her father, but underneath it all Peyton is insecure and scared. She's like every other teenager in this world who wants to blaze a new trail in life but isn't quite sure how to get started.

Further complicated for Peyton is her on-again, off-again relationship with Lucas Scott. She wants to be with Lucas, but she's not sure how close she wants to get.

Peyton puts on a strong, confident facade when she's in public. But when she's at home, she often lets her insecurities get the best of her. At times she feels trapped living in a small town. She wonders if there is a life for her out there beyond Tree Hill.

The trappings of a small town are nothing new for Hilarie Burton, the actress who plays Peyton on *One Tree Hill*. Hilarie was born on July 1, 1982, in Sterling Park, Virginia, to Bill, an antique collector, and Lisa, a real estate agent. Hilarie is the oldest of four children in her family. She has three younger brothers—Billy, Johnny, and Conrad—whom she has affectionately nicknamed Billy Awesome, Johnny Kickass, and C-Rock. For the record, Hilarie's family nicknamed her H-Bomb.

Growing up in a small town had its advantages and disadvantages for Hilarie. On one hand, she knew everyone in her town and they all knew her. On the other hand, there wasn't much to do and, Hilarie says with a laugh, "You knew everyone and everyone knew you."

Still, Hilarie says, "It was a pretty great place to grow up because it was small enough, it was safe, and you had to have an imagination. Yet it was big enough that you didn't have to get into too much trouble to have a good time."

Back in the 1980s, Sterling Park was very rural. There were no shopping malls, no movie theaters, and not a ton of restaurants. Because of this, Hilarie says she and her family "had to be creative. We went to the public library for practically everything. We read a lot, we would get movies and musicals from the library. It was great."

Outdoor sports were also very much a part of Hilarie's childhood. Having three younger brothers, Hilarie became quite a tomboy. She did everything they did, from playing Little League baseball to climbing trees and taking karate lessons. She wasn't into girly-girl rituals like getting her hair braided or painting her fingernails. Instead, it was all about hanging with the boys and having a good time.

"I was not a cute kid," Hilarie declares. "I had really crooked teeth, big frizzy hair, Coke-bottle glasses. I was never about trying to fit in with the girls because the guys were so much more accepting. They were like, 'I don't care if you're not cute, can you run fast? Can you climb a tree?'"

When she wasn't scaling oak trees or skipping stones across a lake, Hilarie spent her free time learning to sing opera music and act in the theater. Her first-ever acting role was as Gretel von Trapp in a local high school production of *The Sound of Music.*

"I auditioned for it. I had to go in and sing a little song and say some lines and I got the part," Hilarie says. "I was so overwhelmed and excited."

Hilarie continued to pursue acting as a preteen and appeared in several regional productions of *Into the Woods, A Midsummer Night's Dream*, and *A Tale of Two Cities.*

A New York–based talent agent saw Hilarie perform and offered to represent her. Hilarie was excited about the possibilities that lay ahead. Her parents could see that she had the drive to succeed, so they happily made the five-hour drive to New York so Hilarie could go on auditions.

"Sometimes my dad would take the day off work to drive me up to New York and back in one day," Hilarie says. "They were super, super supportive of me. They would do anything for me and they never pushed me. They were always saying, 'You want to do it, then do it.' I am so grateful for that."

When she entered junior high school, Hilarie traded in her clunky eyeglasses for contact lenses. She styled her hair and wore cute little preppy outfits. Acting soon took a backseat to student government and cheerleading. She decided to stop auditioning for a while and enjoy being in school and being with her friends.

It all seemed like fun at the time, Hilarie says, until she rekindled her love for the theater by joining the high school drama club.

"Once I did that I kind of dropped the other activities," Hilarie explains.

She knew that she wanted to pursue acting as a career, though she didn't lose her focus on her studies. An A student, Hilarie loved English, math, and science. She knew that the foundation for any career was a solid education.

"All of my friends and I were really academic. I was in all honors classes. Studies never consumed me," Hilarie explains. "But I made straight As. I knew by making good grades I'd be able to go to a good school and get out of Sterling Park."

In the fall of 2000, Hilarie left Sterling Park and went off to college at Fordham University in New York City.

One fall morning, two weeks after moving to the Big Apple, Hilarie was out and about with her roommate near Fordham's Lincoln Center campus when a crowd recruiter for *Total Request Live* approached the two girls. The recruiter was looking for fresh faces to fill the Times Square audience that day. Hilarie was jazzed at the prospect of going to Times Square. She had only been living in the city a short time and thought it would be fun to watch one of MTV's most popular shows film.

Since she was so new to the city, the subway ride from their campus dorm to the studio was an adventure in itself. When Hilarie arrived at the *TRL* studio and took in the cameras, the lights, the music, her heart started racing. That's when Hilarie's adventure began.

A *TRL* production member saw Hilarie in the studio and asked her if she would be interested in taking part in a little contest the show was having that day. The contest was "Who Wants to Be a VJ?" and it involved a spontaneous audition of sorts—interviewing *TRL* host Carson Daly on the air. Hilarie gladly accepted the challenge. After all, she figured she didn't have anything to lose. And what's more, what a fun story this would be to tell her family back home.

Several wannabe VJ contestants took their turns with Carson, each one asking silly questions like "Boxers or briefs?" Hilarie immediately caught on to the playful vibe. When it was her turn, she took things in a more creative direction.

"I got up there and I'm like, 'All right, so you find out you're adopted. Which two rock stars do you pray are your parents?'" Hilarie recounts. "He's like, 'Prince and Debbie Gibson. No question.' So immediately we had a pretty good rapport."

Several more contestants tried out after Hilarie, but it was already a done deal. She was the best and she was going to get to be a VJ for MTV. Little did she know her gig started immediately.

The next night Hilarie joined a *TRL* crew to cover the red carpet arrivals at the Video Music Awards ceremony at Manhattan's Radio City Music Hall. Just two days earlier, Hilarie was an unknown college freshman trying to find her way to classes on the Fordham campus. And now here she was, shoulder to shoulder with experienced camera crews from *Access Hollywood*, *Entertainment Tonight*, and CNN. It was no biggie that this was her first-ever red carpet. Hilarie handled herself like a pro.

She interviewed stars like Macy Gray and Shawn and Marlon Wayans as they arrived in their designer duds for the show. Hilarie held her own until teen divas Britney Spears and Christina Aguilera arrived. When Britney arrived, the crowd went nuts, camera crews scrambled, and Hilarie steadied her nerves. Holding out her microphone, Hilarie vied for Britney's attention, to no avail. Britney and her bodyguards cruised right by without offering even so much as a smile to Hilarie.

Hilarie was bummed but knew she'd tried her best. Or had she? She regrouped and convinced herself that she would try a little harder the next time a big-name celebrity came down the carpet. Sure enough, Christina was stepping out of her limo. Christina's entourage was similar to Britney's. Her bodyguards kept a stern watch on the manic crowds as the young diva made her way toward the music hall entrance. Once again camera crews scrambled to get into place. Hilarie held her microphone out a little farther and yelled a little louder but, as was the case with Britney, Christina and her group walked on by.

The next day Hilarie went back to *TRL* to report on the evening's events to Carson. After a tape rolled of Hilarie's red carpet reporting, Carson decided to engage in a little playful banter. He teased her about not landing interviews with Britney and Christina, the big fish at the awards show.

Hilarie, ever the quick wit, responded, "Whatever, dude. They didn't win anything anyway."

The *TRL* audience roared with approval. Carson and company were so impressed with Hilarie, they offered her a full-time gig, which she happily accepted.

It's ironic to Hilarie that her big break was on an MTV show. After all, she wasn't allowed to watch it when she was in high school.

"Until I started working at MTV, the only concert I'd been to was by the Four Tops and the Temptations," Hilarie says. "I never listened to that kind of music growing up. I was the last person who should have gotten that job. I never wanted to be a television personality, I was an actress."

Hilarie says learning the ropes at the world-famous music network was fast and furious and something she couldn't have done without Carson's help.

"I got taught by the best. I was eased into it. I had Carson as an example," Hilarie says. "It really opened up a lot of doors for me. He saw something in me that other people didn't see and he supported me a lot. He's such a good older-brother figure in the city."

Thanks to MTV's flexible schedule and Hilarie's knack for multitasking, she was able to manage schoolwork and the show. It was quite the heady experience to get to meet some of her favorite stars, like Will Ferrell and Angelina Jolie.

Her major was criminology, but after her freshman year Hilarie switched to journalism. She also transferred to New York University, which is known for its writing and performing arts programs.

Hilarie tried her best to juggle school and work, but because of the demands of the *TRL* schedule, her grades started to slip. She decided to take a leave of absence from her studies because, she explains, "I wanted to do college right."

In 2002, Hilarie got a call that one of her favorite television shows, *Dawson's Creek*, was filming a spring break episode. MTV is known for its terrific on-location spring break specials. The producers of *Dawson's Creek* thought it would be great to have Hilarie play herself as an MTV VJ in a scene involving the *Dawson's* gang on break.

The experience was all Hilarie needed to get the wheels turning in her head. She had always wanted to be an actress, and the *Dawson's Creek* episode was the perfect push toward expanding her career. Hilarie hired an agent, who was able to alert television and film casting directors that the young MTV star was also an aspiring actress.

Hilarie's first big audition was for the movie *Radio*. She was considered for the role of Ed Harris's daughter in the 2003 movie.

"I auditioned and went for callback after callback after callback," Hilarie explains. "I talked to Mike Tollin, one of the producers on the movie, and we had a difference of opinion about the character. He wanted her to be a bit more dependent on her father's love and I wanted her to be stronger. I didn't get the part, and I was really bummed about it. I was like, 'Man, I should learn to play by other people's rules.' I thought if I stood up for myself they'd agree with me.'"

Hilarie was kicking herself about not getting the role. Little did she know that she actually had managed to capture the producer's attention. A few months later, she got another call from Mike Tollin, who was an executive producer on *One Tree Hill*. He remembered Hilarie's *Radio* audition and thought she'd be a good fit for the role of cheerleader Peyton Sawyer. Hilarie read the part on tape, which was in turn sent to *OTH* creator Mark Schwahn. He agreed—Hilarie was just the actress they were looking for.

"I never even planned on doing TV. I was auditioning for films predominantly and I was really looking forward to getting involved in more film work and then this script came along and I read it and I was like, 'I have to be this girl,'" Hilarie says.

Hilarie loved that she was getting to play Peyton, a cheerleader who looks like she's all together. She's got great looks, she's popular in school, and she's dating the hot school jock. But underneath, Peyton is unsure of her footing. She's trying to find out who she is while she's pretending to be who she thinks she should be. Peyton's inner conflicts reminded Hilarie of her high school days.

"I can really relate to the role. She was me in high school. I was on the cheerleading squad. And I was very bitter about it," Hilarie confesses. "I know what it is to be a girl who hates the popularity game."

To better prepare herself for the role, Hilarie did a little digging into her own past. "I went back and I got all my old journals from high school and I was reading through them. Just how tormented I was, and so the character is very much like how I was in high school. So to be able to go back and see where my head was at the time and bring it to the show is a lot of fun."

Just because Hilarie landed an acting gig didn't mean she was going to give up her day job, so to speak. That is, Hilarie now has two day jobs! Hilarie worried about the prospect of having to leave *TRL*. She loved the show so much and she didn't want to leave, but at the same time she was really psyched about landing the role on *OTH*. Hilarie, ever the multitasker, chose both shows.

"I can't complain," Hilarie says. "Nothing about my career has been difficult. I mean, I walked into the MTV offices and they were like, 'Do you want a full-time job as a VJ?' And I was like, 'Yeah, as long as it doesn't mess up my acting career.'"

During the first season of *OTH*, Hilarie shot from Monday to Thursday in Wilmington, then flew up to New York City on Friday to tape *TRL*, returning to Wilmington on Saturday afternoon. Even though it was a grueling, exhausting schedule, Hilarie found herself incredibly fulfilled. She felt as though she had won the lottery with her two very successful television shows.

"Of course when I got the job at *One Tree Hill* and I was juggling *TRL*, it wasn't ideal, it wasn't typical," Hilarie says. "I guess I could have looked at it like, 'Oh man, I'm so tired. I'm so worn out.' But I looked at it like, 'Man, the grass is greener on the other side and I own both backyards right now.' I'm not happy unless I'm really busy."

What's more, it wasn't just about the work. It was about the people. Hilarie had made many new friends in New York and Wilmington.

"I can go up to New York and see my friends and go out at night and enjoy the city and then I come back to Wilmington and have this nice little quiet, small-town existence. I'm pretty lucky," Hilarie says.

"It's not bad. A lot of people are like, 'Oh, you have to go back and forth every week.' But flight time is my alone time. I appreciate it. I love it. I sleep," Hilarie explains. "It's busy. You're on set all day long with, like, a lot of people.

We have huge casts and so there's a ton of people around at all times. So the flight time, my alone time—I can read a book or just knit or do all the nerdy things I like to do by myself—is very appreciated."

It doesn't happen often, but when Hilarie does find herself with a free weekend or several days off in a row, she's likely to indulge her inner shopper. Around the Wilmington area Hilarie has found a treasure trove of collectibles at antique stores.

"I like animal parts, skulls, things that are just a little bit weird," Hilarie says. "I've found hunting bundles, bows and arrows. I like having things no one else has."

Her eclectic collection has grown over the past year, and it's made her Wilmington digs feel more like home. Often Hilarie is just as content shopping at a home improvement warehouse as she would be for a new outfit. She recently finished putting crown molding in her house and did some light landscaping in the yard. She also built, sanded, and stained a bed for herself. No doubt Hilarie could afford to hire someone to do the work for her. But she enjoys the satisfaction of starting a project and following it through to the end.

"I've always been into it," she says. "This is my house. I'm a big girl."

Hilarie is a big girl and at 22, she's got big plans for her future. While she's certainly happy with her life today,

Hilarie is constantly looking for new challenges and adventures. She enjoys writing and hopes to someday have one of her own pieces produced and performed. She also hopes to one day have a family of her own. Because she travels so much for work, Hilarie has developed a little hobby to keep herself amused.

"Every city I go to I like to get a book on its local ghost stories," she says. "I anticipate going on a car trip with my kids (someday) and no matter where we are, I'll be able to tell them a story and freak them out. I'll be that mom the other kids won't be allowed around."

CHAPTER SEVEN

Sophia Bush Is
Brooke Davis

Brooke Davis wants to have it all and puts on a front that she does indeed have it all. The beautiful, popular cheerleader seemingly gets whatever she wants. Deep down, though, she's not sure what she wants—and what's more, she doesn't want to admit that to herself, let alone her friends. Instead Brooke puts on her "life of the party" persona and lets loose. She tends to keep the struggles she faces and the hurt she feels locked up inside.

"I knew girls like her. I think women run to being validated by guys when they don't feel good about themselves," Sophia says. "What I loved about Brooke and what I read from her at the beginning, this girl acts like she's so confident and she's just not. She's not sure of herself at all and it's sort of tragic at times. That's what I love about playing the character."

Sophia was born on July 8, 1982, in Pasadena, California,

to Charles, a photographer, and Maureen, a photography studio manager.

Even though Pasadena is a short freeway ride away from Los Angeles, it has a small-town feel to it. Downtown Pasadena is a shopping and dining mecca. But the residential areas feature beautifully landscaped neighborhoods and spacious parks.

"It was a great place to grow up," Sophia says. "It was so beautiful and green and residential. We were close enough to the city and I know it really well, but I definitely got to have a little more of a pure childhood."

Sophia developed a very outgoing personality as a young girl. She attributes that mostly to the fact that she was an only child and had to be proactive about meeting people and making friends. When she was a young girl, Sophia often accompanied her father while he worked on commercial photo shoots. She engaged in conversation with the other adults who were working with her father with relative ease.

"I was never shy," Sophia says. "I was actually the kid who never stopped talking."

As a kid growing up around the industry, Sophia could have gotten into acting or modeling if she wanted to. Her parents strongly encouraged her to refrain from working while she was young. They spent all their time with models and actresses and they knew that the demands and the stress of the industry is a lot for a young kid to handle. They wanted Sophia to enjoy her childhood and then when she was older she could make a more informed decision about her career path.

"I can't thank them enough for that," Sophia says.

During elementary school Sophia enjoyed playing sports, hanging out with her friends, and reading. She attended Pasadena's Westridge School, an exclusive all-girls private school. Students followed a strict dress code and academics and cultural enrichment were stressed. The school has a small class size to ensure its students get as much individualized attention as possible. This also helped Sophia bond with her fellow classmates and make a small, tight-knit circle of friends.

"My parents were strict with me, in terms of giving me my work ethic," Sophia says. "But they are the coolest. They always encouraged me to pursue my dreams and they said anything was possible as long as I was willing to work hard for it."

In eighth grade Sophia performed in her first school play. Even though she doesn't remember the project, she does recall that this initial experience hooked her for good.

"Right after I did that play I knew I wanted to do more theater. I knew it was for me and it took me in a whole new direction," Sophia says. "It was so far from what I thought I wanted to do. I was thinking of being a pediatrician.

I wanted to work with kids. But I fell into acting and I fell in love with it."

Westridge boasts an advanced drama department and Sophia immersed herself in the school's theater program. During her high school years, Sophia credits her drama director, Tim Wright, for being "such a mentor for me. He taught me so much and I'm so grateful to him."

Sophia performed in five and sometimes six shows each year while at Westridge. Her favorite production was a play titled *Last Chance, Texaco*. It was about three women—one who is crossing the United States and stops at a gas station that a mother and daughter run together. The dialogue is about these three women and how they are wary of one another initially. But they are forced to spend a day together and at the end find that they aren't really all that different from one another.

"It was an exceptional piece. Our productions at school were really heavy," Sophia says. "We did great funny plays, too. But my favorites were the heavier dramas."

When Sophia was a senior in high school, she met a Hollywood manager by the name of Joan Green. Joan saw one of Sophia's performances and invited her to come to her office for a meeting. She thought Sophia was talented enough to break into television and film. Sophia met with Joan, who began sending her on film and television auditions. Meanwhile, of course, Sophia had to concentrate on school.

After graduating from Westridge in June 2000, Sophia enrolled at the University of Southern California. The university is located in downtown Los Angeles and is one of the country's finest academic institutions. Sophia decided to major in journalism at USC.

"It was a wonderful place to learn and study," Sophia says, laughing. "As social as I am, I've always kind of been this nerdy bookworm when it comes to school. I've always loved school and I've loved learning. USC was wonderful because it gave me the best of both worlds. They have this great football team, so there was always something to do on the weekends. Plus, I had the best that academics has to offer."

Sophia lived in the USC dormitory for a semester before moving to an off-campus apartment with some friends. It was the first time Sophia had lived on her own and she found the experience to be "fun and strange. No one was there regulating your behavior so you have to learn to be self-sufficient, and I was very lucky to have the high school experience I did because it gave me a lot of discipline."

Sophia enjoyed learning about journalism yet she still wanted to indulge her acting passion. "I went out on a few auditions just to see how things would be and kind of get comfortable with the environment," Sophia says.

In 2001 Sophia auditioned for the film *Van Wilder*. She initially read for one of the main character parts and the casting director thought Sophia did a great audition. That was the good news. The bad news was that Sophia looked too young to play opposite the lead actor. Even though she was 18, on screen she looked like she was 14 or 15.

A week later the casting director contacted Sophia and told her that she had another role for her in the movie if she was interested.

"I was like, 'Of course I would!' So that was the start of it all," Sophia says. "It didn't freak me out or overwhelm me being on a set for the first time. I went in and I did my work and I had a really good time. I was lucky to have that as a starting point because everyone on the film was wonderful. The director was awesome and the cast was cool. They all put me totally at ease."

Even though it was a small role, Sophia was blown away by how many people began to recognize her on the street. One of the movie's scenes seems to have become a fan favorite.

"I come in at the end of the movie and throw a wrench in between Ryan Reynolds's and Tara Reid's characters," Sophia explains. "He decides to make out with the freshman girl (played by Sophia) down the hall that's totally in love with him — it's totally a crisis point in the movie and people still stop me on the street to tell me that they liked it. It blows me away."

Sophia could have dropped out of school to pursue acting full-time, but it was important to her to earn a degree. She continued to audition when she had time, always making sure that acting didn't interfere with her academic schedule.

She acted in an independent student film and later landed the part of Ray Liotta's daughter in the HBO movie *Point of Origin*. Sophia is rarely at a loss for words, but when she found out she was going to work with the star of *Goodfellas* — one of her all-time favorite movies — she was practically speechless. After a few days of working together, Sophia got up her nerve to tell Ray how much she enjoyed his work.

"I was like, 'I loved you in *Goodfellas*,' and he was like, 'Are you serious?'" Sophia recalls. "I think he was surprised to hear that from such a young person, but he thought it was awesome and cool. It was so amazing to work with him because he's got such intensity. He's so talented. To be around him and do all of my scenes for him was a great experience for me."

The next big job for Sophia was the feature film *Terminator 3*. Sophia was cast in the leading female role and she was thrilled to work with star Arnold Schwarzenegger. But soon after filming began (the movie was shot in 2002 and released in 2003) the producers realized they made a mistake. They loved working with Sophia, but they felt after viewing her performance on film that she ultimately didn't look mature enough for the role. Claire Danes, a more mature-looking young actress, was brought in to replace Sophia. The experience was frustrating for Sophia, who had done nothing wrong at all.

"I've been told, 'Oh, you're too young' so many times in my career," Sophia says. "It's to the point where I just now can play a 16-year-old and I'm now 22. So at 19 years old they tried to make me look 26 and it just didn't work and that's nobody's fault. It just happens. Everybody there was great about it so it's no big deal."

Sophia had one more year left at USC, but she couldn't resist auditioning for the part of Brooke Davis on *One Tree Hill.* The role was appealing to Sophia because she's always been a fan of the drama genre and with the character Brooke, there's a lot of drama and a little bit of sarcastic comedy.

"Brooke is made of so much flash, but in reality it's all a mask to cover up a girl's insecurities. It's a false confidence and there's something poignant to that," Sophia explains.

The first audition was for creator Mark Schwahn. Then Sophia was asked back to read for several more producers and studio and network executives.

When Sophia learned that she had been offered the part, she couldn't turn it down even though it meant that she would have to take a leave of absence from USC. The school was completely understanding about Sophia's situation and granted her request without reservation. When the show ends, Sophia says she plans to finish the rest of her college studies and get that diploma she's worked so hard toward.

With that dilemma solved, Sophia found herself faced with another one — having to move to Wilmington, North Carolina, where *One Tree Hill* is shot.

"Moving here was very hard," Sophia says. "I remember walking to get on the plane and leaving my family and my friends. That was really hard. But getting here and getting to know everybody and getting to know this place, it suddenly became very easy."

Sophia became very close very fast with her fellow costars. Because of the first season's intensive shooting schedule, the group rehearsed and worked together for many hours. They discovered that not only did they like working together but also that they genuinely liked one another as individuals. The girls got together regularly for coffee or lunch while the guys connected over snacks and football. Real life soon imitated art when Sophia and Chad, whose characters became involved, discovered they had feelings for each other.

For a time Chad and Sophia kept their relationship under wraps for fear that it might make some of the folks on the show uncomfortable. But their love for each other grew deeper and one night at dinner they spilled the beans. Everyone was ecstatic for them.

In the summer of 2004, Sophia filmed the movie *Supercross* in Los Angeles and Las Vegas. She plays Zoe Lang, a law student who discovers the sport of motocross when she becomes involved with a rider named K.C. Carlyle (played by actor Steve Howey).

During that same summer, Sophia traveled three times to Australia to visit with Chad, who was there filming the horror flick *House of Wax*. One evening Chad asked Sophia to marry him in very romantic fashion. Just before sundown, Chad lit dozens of candles and presented Sophia with roses and a beautiful ring. Chad also had a special, but private, message for Sophia spelled out in lights on the tennis court of the house where he was staying. Sophia was moved to tears by Chad's romantic overtures. And of course she said yes!

"My relationship with Chad is very special," Sophia says. "I could talk to you for hours about why our relationship

The cast of *One Tree Hill* — Sophia Bush as Brooke Davis, Chad Michael Murray as Lucas Scott, Hilarie Burton as Peyton Sawyer, James Lafferty as Nathan Scott, and Bethany Joy Lenz as Haley James.

Chad has a lot in common with his character: "I've got a distinct advantage because it happened to me."

Like his character on the show, James was a basketball star in high school.

Hilarie divides her time between two big parts — Peyton on *One Tree Hill* and a VJ on MTV's *TRL*.

Unlike her character on *OTH*, Sophia worked very hard in high school: "I've always kind of been this nerdy bookworm when it comes to school."

Bethany says one of her favorite things about her character, Haley, is that she doesn't want to be like everyone else.

True love, on-screen and off: Chad and Sophia became engaged to be married during the summer of 2004.

James and Bethany are husband and wife on the show, but offscreen they're just good friends.

Sophia and Hilarie hang out together even when the cameras aren't rolling. "We genuinely enjoy each other's company," says Sophia.

A tangled web of intrigue on TV
— and friendship in real life.

is great and why I love him. But I don't feel our personal life is anyone's business but our own."

Going back to Wilmington for the show's second season was exciting for everyone. The cast and crew couldn't wait to reunite and share stories of how they spent their summer breaks. More importantly, there was a great deal of anticipation about how the show would continue to evolve.

"A lot of Brooke's bravado got stripped away through season one," Sophia explains. "Her insecurities started coming out. She's back to hiding them and really guarding herself because she was hurt so badly by her first real love. I'm looking forward to her battling with the new walls she has put up around her heart, seeing how long they can really last."

One thing that is certain to last is the friendships Sophia has made while working on *One Tree Hill*.

"We have a family here," Sophia says. "We all hang out at each other's houses, we go to the movies, dinner, play football on the weekends. All of us genuinely enjoy each other's company. I feel so incredibly lucky that I get to go to work and do what I love every day. It's amazing."

CHAPTER EIGHT

Bethany Lenz
Is Haley James

Everybody should be lucky enough to have a friend like Haley James. Haley is the kind of girl who can get along with the popular kids, the jocks, and the introverts. In fact, her best friend, Lucas Scott, is one of the more reserved kids at Tree Hill High. Haley is a rock for Lucas. She's one of his most loyal supporters. But she can't help falling for Lucas's half brother, Nathan.

Haley can stand on her own two feet in a crowd, but one-on-one, she's still a fragile young girl. It's precisely those qualities that drew actress Bethany Lenz to the character. Bethany, it turns out, has a few things in common with Haley. Both are quick-witted, both are wise beyond their years, and both can hold their own in just about any situation.

"Her vulnerability is more attractive to me than a girl that is self-reliant," Bethany says.

Bethany Joy Lenz was born on April 2, 1981 in Hollywood, Florida. While it wasn't *the* Hollywood, maybe there was still something special in the air that influenced Bethany's interests toward entertainment.

When she was four, Bethany's family moved to Arlington, Texas, where she first became acquainted with the theater.

"I was a really energetic kid," Bethany says. "My mom recommended I take some dance classes or some acting classes or something. Once I started doing theater and found this outlet for my energy, it sparked a real interest and I kept doing it."

While attending Pope Elementary, seven-year-old Bethany starred as a munchkin in an Arlington's Creative Arts Theater production of *The Wizard of Oz*.

Bethany had a knack for performing and her parents took great pleasure in seeing her thrive onstage. They encouraged her to explore the theater. A few years later, Bethany starred as Scout in *To Kill a Mockingbird* at the Irving Community Theater near her hometown. After attending Dallas TV and Film Workshop for a year, Bethany was invited to travel with a small group to Los Angeles during pilot season. While there, Bethany landed her first professional gig—a commercial for the teen series *Swan's Crossing*.

After her visit to Los Angeles, Bethany auditioned for *The Mickey Mouse Club* in Texas. Bethany's mom had been reading a book written by a New York talent agent. She phoned the agent and told her about Bethany. The agent agreed that if Bethany made it to at least the final round of auditions, then she would meet with her when the family moved to the New York area.

Bethany made it to the final round of auditions and found a New York–based agent, Nancy Carlson, who was eager to work with her.

After settling in Wildwood, New Jersey, Bethany met with Nancy, who promptly sent her to a number of commercial, theater, and television auditions.

"Eventually," Bethany explains, "in any city, if you keep going long enough, casting agents and talent directors get to know you and they keep bringing you in for things."

Being an only child, Bethany often spent her free time reading, playing guitar or piano, or painting and drawing to indulge her active, creative side. She enjoyed taking gymnastics classes and dance classes to train her body. She concentrated on becoming a better vocalist and developed an impressive four-octave vocal range.

"I trained with a man named Richard Barrett, who is the director of the Brooklyn College of Opera," Bethany says proudly. "He's trained me since I was 13. He taught me everything I ever wanted to sing and I'm grateful to him for sharing so much of his musical wisdom with me."

She also started to write poetry and music, and delved into books that fed her mind. Bethany says that although she had a very nice group of friends in school, she wasn't challenged in the classroom—except for a few select teachers.

Bethany says of her disinterest in school, for example, "I think when you're in a public school and the teachers have 20 kids in a class—they all learn differently. I'm always a better learner one-on-one. Take science, for example, which is so technical sometimes. But when we went outside into the field and took nature walks and the teacher would talk about the different species of plants or frogs and I could actually see them, touch them, and smell them—then I could connect."

Bethany continued pursuing theater and music and soon landed a couple of national commercials for Eggo Waffles and Dr Pepper. In 1996, Bethany was cast as a cheerleader daughter in the Stephen King horror film *Thinner*. It was a big leap for Bethany.

While a junior at Eastern Christian High School, Bethany got her big break in show business when she was cast for nine episodes on the soap opera *Guiding Light*. The soap, the longest-running daytime drama, was shot in nearby New York City.

Bethany was thrilled about working on such a popular, fun show. She was cast as the teenage clone of Reva Shayne. Landing the role came as a shocker to Bethany, mostly because she looked nothing like Kim Zimmer, the actress who originally played the character. Kim was blond-haired and blue-eyed. Bethany had brown eyes and a much darker shade of blond hair.

But producers told Bethany to wait and see. After the makeup department finished with Bethany, she was surprised to see how they were able to make her look like a young Kim Zimmer.

"They had me wear blue contacts and they lightened my hair a little bit and it worked," Bethany says.

Not only did Bethany look the part, she performed it extremely well. When her storyline ended, she was sad to go. And for *Guiding Light* producers, the feeling was mutual. That's why eight months later, when another young female character was being cast, Bethany was at the top of their list.

While it doesn't happen often in primetime television, in soap operas actors can be cast to play multiple characters on the same show. What's more, different actors are often hired to play existing characters. Such was the case with the Michelle Bauer role, which had previously been portrayed by actresses Rachel Miner (who later married

Macaulay Culkin) and Rebecca Bunting (Greenley on *All My Children*).

Sure, fans might have remembered Bethany's turn as Reva. But eight months and a lot of story arcs had passed. Michelle was described as the ultimate girl next door, but over the next two years the character evolved into a mafia princess.

Some days Bethany was required to perform thirty pages of dialogue, which is quite a workload for any actor. Bethany credits her ability to memorize all of her lines to a "photographic memory. I go over the script the night before, kind of analyzing it and taking notes. Sometimes I'd run it with my friends," she says matter-of-factly. To this day, the technique serves her well.

Bethany jumped into the role of Michelle while she was a senior at East Christian, which meant she had to be home-schooled and tutored in order to keep up with her classwork.

"My senior year I was not really connected to high school," Bethany says. "Quite honestly, I couldn't wait to get out of there. I really enjoy learning, don't get me wrong, but I wasn't really a social butterfly. I kind of did my own thing. I had friends I hung out with, but I never felt like I was a part of the crowd. I had only two or three close friends in high school. The people I was closest to were on the soap at that point, so I went to school when I felt like it. If I got bored I'd go down to the art studio and do pottery. I didn't go crazy, but I pretty much did whatever I wanted."

Most actors would hold on to their steady job for as long as they could. But Bethany was looking ahead at the bigger picture. As the end of her two-year contract on *Guiding Light* neared, she had hoped to either study at London's prestigious Royal Academy of Dramatic Arts or take a year off before pursuing a college degree.

In 1999, soon after her high school graduation, Bethany was cast in the ABC television movie *Mary and Rhoda*. The film was the first time legendary actresses Mary Tyler Moore and Valerie Harper had worked together since their hit sitcom, *The Mary Tyler Moore Show*, went off the air in 1974.

Bethany was cast to play Mary Tyler Moore's opinionated daughter, Rose Cronin, a New York University film student. The movie aired in February 2000 and was a ratings smash for ABC, pulling in nearly 18 million viewers. The primetime movie was great exposure for Bethany, who went on to land steady guest-starring roles for the next couple of years in TV shows like *Off Centre*, *Charmed*, *Felicity*, and *Maybe It's Me*.

In 2003, Bethany shot the cheerleading film *Bring It On Again*. In the movie she plays a bratty cheerleader named Marni Potts. The role was a completely new adventure for Bethany, who was never a cheerleader in real life. She enjoyed the athleticism involved in portraying a cheerleader, and she enjoyed acting like a bit of a lunatic, especially in a scene she shared with actress Bree Turner. Of the experience, Bethany remembers, "It gave me a chance to let out the madwoman in me. It was really fun."

After the movie wrapped, Bethany was on the lookout for her next role. She went on to land guest-starring roles in *Charmed, Felicity,* and *Maybe It's Me.* In between filming, Bethany kept up her presence in the LA theater scene. She worked with the director Arthur Allan Sidleman on a musical version of the classic teen novel *The Outsiders.* And she also had the opportunity to work with Garry Marshall and musical directors Carole King and Paul Williams on a musical workshop written by Mr. Marshall.

Soon afterward, Bethany landed a two-episode role in *The Guardian.* The *OTH* pilot had already been shot when Bethany was called in to read for the producers.

"Haley was just another random audition that I went in for," Bethany says of how she got the role. "There was someone else who filmed the pilot, but the show just wanted to take (the character) in a different direction."

The role appealed to Bethany for several reasons. The character of Haley is a girly-girl but not a pushover. Haley isn't afraid to speak her mind but also knows when it's time to listen.

"I really liked that she was a light," Bethany says. "I felt that there was an innocence to her that wasn't a naiveté—she chose to be innocent. I really appreciated that because there are characters in this medium that are portrayed as innocent and it's because they don't know any better. I liked that Haley says, 'I don't want to be like everyone else.' I really connected with that mentality. So when the part came in and I read through it, I thought, Wow, this is really funny and great. I went in and I read with Chad and we just hit it off. I felt really uninhibited with the character because I felt like I knew her so well."

The relationship between Haley and Lucas has been compared to Joey and Dawson's friendship on *Dawson's Creek*. Bethany says the challenge of making the *OTH* characters' friendship unique is what good television is all about.

"I read somewhere that there are only really seven stories that can be told, it just depends on how you tell it. I loved *Dawson's Creek*, and it's not like those stories weren't told on *90210*, but *Dawson's* was a new way to tell those stories. And that's why it's great to do our show. We get to relate to teenagers and show things that teenagers have been going through on TV for decades but told in a different way."

When Bethany learned she had gotten the role of Haley, she was excited about moving to Wilmington, but thought it would be difficult to move away from her family and friends. But soon she and her cat, Pisa, set up camp and fit right in.

"I love Wilmington," Bethany enthuses. "It's very country and beachy. I don't miss Los Angeles, I just miss my friends there."

But Bethany is happy that she's had the chance to make new friends at *OTH*. "We're close. You're forced to be close when you are put in a bubble and all of your friends and family are a six-hour plane ride away. It's been everything you'd expect with a group of opposite personalities all on one set. There's been love, there's drama, there's tears and ten times as much laughter, but we always pull through," Bethany says, noting that she and costar Hilarie Burton have developed a fabulous friendship. "She's got such a great heart. She's a great friend."

When it comes to downtime, Bethany is content with good food, good conversation, or, if she's alone, a good book. She indulges her creative side with music, photography, and writing. When it comes to her social life — dating — she says it is much less of a struggle as it was when she was in high school.

"I definitely struggled with boys," Bethany says of her teen years. "At that age you're just discovering what it's like to have crush on a boy and have him like you back. It's just like, 'How do I even deal with this?'"

She says she deals with dating by being true to her heart. "It's a precious thing and not everyone deserves it. Hold on to it. Stick to your guns and don't let anyone tell you that your standards are too high."

As *OTH* enters its second season, Bethany says it's up to the producers and the writers what will happen next. For example, if Haley had to choose, would she pick Lucas or Nathan? "I secretly picture Haley going off and coming back in season five with some European man that just takes everyone off guard," Bethany says, laughing.

In real life Bethany is just as imaginative. When she thinks about what she would be doing if she wasn't acting, she says honestly, "I have no idea." She admits that at 23, she's got a long road ahead of her. Acting, she says, might not be the end-all, be-all.

"I still don't know what I'm going to be," she says. "I love acting. I would love to be an English teacher. I would love to be a housewife and have a chateau in the south of France. I would love to be a singer that travels to cafes around different towns or open a boulangerie or patisserie near my family and ride horses, have kids, and just enjoy living."

One thing's for sure—with Bethany the possibilities are endless.

"Right now, I am loving my life and can't wait to see where it goes," she says. "It's exciting."

CHAPTER NINE

Moira Kelly Is Karen Roe

For the past 16 years, Karen Roe has had to endure many obstacles. She's a single mom who's raising a teenage son, Lucas, in the small town of Tree Hill. Only in her mid-thirties, Karen has undergone much public scrutiny over her teenage pregnancy. Still, she's managed to build a solid family unit with her son. Now that Lucas is a young adult, Karen is in a period of self-discovery. She realizes that the dreams she was forced to put on hold for so many years are perhaps still attainable.

Actress Moira (pronounced MOY-rah) Kelly went through a period of discovery when she read for the role of Karen Roe.

"I've never been shy about playing a mother or playing an older role," Moira says. "To me, it's always playing the best role I can get and one that would challenge me. My only concern at the time was I wasn't sure if people would believe I was the mother of a teenage boy."

The more Moira let herself sink into the role and look through Karen's eyes, the more she knew that it was indeed believable for a young woman to raise a teenage son on her own.

Moira is one of six kids raised on Long Island, New York, by her Irish immigrant parents. Her father, Peter, was a professional violin player and her mother, Anne, was a nurse. Even though she grew up in a neighborhood where most of the kids talk with heavy accents, Moira says she and her siblings never acquired a New York drawl. Her parents, she says, were very conscientious about making sure the kids spoke proper English.

"My father was very strict about diction and speaking correctly," Moira says, laughing. "None of us have that distinctive Long Island accent."

Music was a big part of Moira's childhood. Not only did her father play the violin but also her mother played piano. All of the kids learned to play instruments at one point or another.

"We were all introduced to music at a very early age. My father used to tour in Ireland with an orchestra every summer and we used to go with him. I was playing the violin at the age of five," Moira says. "I played violin, drums, and piano."

When Moira entered junior high school, she discovered musical theater. She fell in love with being able to sing and dance and act—all at once. She found her interest in music giving way to the theater. Moira's first role onstage was as the back of a cow in a school production of *Gypsy*. But she hardly considers that her big break.

"My first big, big role was Grace Farrell in *Annie* in high school," Moira says. "I fell madly in love with the live audience and decided that was what I was going to go study."

After graduating from Connetquot High School in 1986, Moira enrolled in New York's Marymount College, where she studied theater. During her senior year at college, the theater department invited talent agents to attend a performance showcase. Moira caught one agent's eye, who asked her to come in and meet with his staff. She did and was signed to the agency.

In 1992 Moira's career took off thanks to her performance in the hit film *The Cutting Edge*. In it, Moira played one half of an ice-skating duo who work together to make the Olympic team. The movie is a perfect blend of inspiration and romance. Because the film has a timeless quality about it, Moira's fan base spans generations.

"It was one of MGM's biggest films of that year," Moira says. "Because it is a film that generations of girls will watch, I've been approached by seven-year-old girls who have seen *The Cutting Edge* for the first time and I've been approached by 30-year-olds who saw it when it first came out. I'm amazed at how often that film plays on television."

Moira became a hot commodity in Hollywood. She soon landed two roles in the Robert Downey Jr. feature film *Chaplin*, based on the life of silent-film star Charlie Chaplin. Moira played a young love of Chaplin's named Hetty Kelly, and later in the film she plays Chaplin's wife Oona. The movie received many critical accolades, including an Oscar nomination for Downey Jr.

The year continued to be a big one for Moira, as she starred in *Twin Peaks: Fire Walk with Me*, a big-screen spin-off of the television series *Twin Peaks*.

Other notable roles for Moira include the films *With Honors* and *The Tie That Binds*, and television movies like *Monday After the Miracle* and *To Have and To Hold*.

Over the years Moira has also done extensive voiceover work for audio books and as an adult Nala in the animated feature film *The Lion King*.

In the year 2000, Moira was working on *The West Wing*. She played political consultant Mandy Hampton on the White House drama. After she finished her run, she got married to Steven Hewitt, a Texas businessman.

The birth of her first child, daughter Ella, came in 2001. At that time Moira made a very un-Hollywood move—she decided to take two years off from the business. Some would call a decision like that career suicide, but Moira didn't care. For her, family was the most important thing in the world. She didn't want to miss out on her daughter's first years.

After two years, Moira talked with her agent, her manager, and most important, her husband, about resuming her career. They all agreed she should go to Los Angeles to take some meetings to see what projects were out there.

"I did the pilot season and when I went in to read for *One Tree Hill*, I had thought it was for a movie. I didn't realize it was for a TV series," Moira explains, noting that she has always had an aversion to taking on a full-time TV series role because she never wanted to be locked into playing one character for too long.

"My agent was like, 'You do realize it's a TV show,'" Moira says, laughing. "I was like, 'Oh, well, okay.'"

Moira read for the producers and was offered the role, which she gladly accepted.

"We said, 'Let's go for it and see where it goes,'" Moira says of weighing the decision with her husband.

Like the other actors, Moira was a little hesitant about moving to Wilmington. She and Steven and Ella had been living in Austin, Texas, and had hoped that her next job would move them somewhat closer to a big city.

During the first season, Moira had a few adjustments to make. Professionally, she was playing a woman in her mid-thirties who has a teenage son. Moira was able to draw upon her own experiences with motherhood and her relationship with her mother. But what Moira didn't know until after she arrived in Wilmington was that actor Chad Michael Murray didn't really have a relationship with his mother when he was growing up. Moira and Chad spoke about their onscreen relationship and how they could make it feel genuine and believable for the viewers.

"For Chad and me, what's nice is it's not a very touchy-feely mom-and-son relationship, it's almost a matter of mutual respect," Moira says. "He's not used to being close to a mother figure, but I think it plays off nicely. We come across as Karen and Lucas, who have this mutual understanding where they respect each other, but she still is the authoritative figure in the household. I think people really pick up on that. I have been approached by a lot of older women who tell me they love the relationship between our characters. Whatever it is that Chad feels when we're doing scenes together and whatever it is that I'm playing off of him — so far it seems to work."

Moira's other adjustment was personal. She was pregnant when the show began filming in July 2003. It didn't serve the character well to be pregnant, so Moira had to hide her belly during work.

"I was really nervous because I've never worked pregnant before," Moira explains. "You're kind of limited in how much movement you have and where you can stand or walk. It was funny watching the production every month try to find something else they could hide me behind as I got bigger."

In November 2003, Moira gave birth to her second child, son Eamon. His name is Gaelic for Edward, a nod to both her Irish heritage and her husband's grandfather's name.

Moira took a five-week maternity leave from the show, conveniently at the same time that her character, Karen, went off to Italy.

"I felt like I was pregnant forever. I told Mark [Schwahn, *OTH*'s creator], if anything, please don't make me pregnant this season," Moira jokes.

The camaraderie between the actors—young and old—has only made Moira feel that much more comfortable with her decision to join *OTH*. She's been in the industry long enough to know when she's in a good place personally and professionally. At times, Moira says, she just can't help but lend a bit of advice to her younger costars.

"They are wonderful," Moira says of Chad, James, Hilarie, Sophia, and Bethany Joy. "Some of them are getting a lot at a very young age and they need to be careful. Sometimes I'll say something like, 'Be careful. Your reputation precedes you,' just to kind of give them a little information. You know, it all seems like everything is in their court right now, but this industry is so fickle. I tell them when the next big thing comes up, if they don't have a good reputation or a good body of work or they aren't reliable, they probably won't work again."

Her advice is cautionary, but Moira applauds the young group for having their priorities straight, especially James Lafferty, the youngest *OTH* cast member.

"He is just the sweetest kid and he's handled all this so well, especially living on his own for the first time. He hasn't let any of this get to him at all. I think that's a testament to his family. He's a real kid," Moira says.

Once reluctant to move, Moira now finds herself a happy citizen of Wilmington. Most of the time when she has a day off she's at home or at the park with the kids. She also loves puttering in the garden and painting. Her violin is with her wherever she goes and she enjoys playing every chance she gets.

The Wilmington social scene is a treat for Moira, too. Every week she and Steven get a sitter and go out on a date night.

"We go to dinner, see a movie," Moira says. "But most of my free time is spent with the kids. That's the great thing about this job—it offers me a lot of time to be at home. I work maybe two or three days a week, which is a really wonderful situation to be in, so we're really happy. The kids are my favorite things in the whole world. There's nothing that comes before them."

"When we got here, the first few months it was getting used to the slower, quieter lifestyle," Moira says. "Now that we have two children, we appreciate it so much more. We realize it's a much easier life. I hope the show has many more seasons."

CHAPTER TEN

CHAPTER TEN

Craig Sheffer Is Keith Scott

Being the brother to one of Tree Hill's more prominent citizens hasn't exactly been easy for Keith Scott. He's troubled by his brother's arrogance and disregard for others' needs. When Dan abandoned his pregnant high school sweetheart and chose to accept a college scholarship, Keith stepped in. He helped Karen raise her son, Lucas, and in the process, developed more than platonic feelings for her. But his struggles with feeling inferior to Dan and doing the right thing cloud his actions, putting him in a constant state of angst.

Actor Craig Sheffer plays *One Tree Hill* garage mechanic Keith Scott. Craig has generally opted more for film work as opposed to television work because of the variety of parts and the fact that as an actor, he's not locked into one character for a long period of time. But there was something special about *One Tree Hill*.

"I really liked the blue-collar aspect of it because it's kind of like where I'm from," Craig says. "It's like the world I grew up in, in York, Pennsylvania. It's down-to-earth people and I really liked that aspect. Plus, I'm an athlete and I came from a football town, so that was similar. It was so well written and it had a lot of real emotion to it."

As for the role of Keith, Craig says, "I loved the character. He's like a mentor, he's got a lot of depth, he's emotionally in touch. He's a strong character."

Growing up in York, Craig says he and his older brother, Hogan, were always encouraged to pursue their dreams. "We come from a small town and our neighborhood is even smaller," Craig explains. "My parents always said, 'You can be whatever you want to be.' I totally believed that I could be president if I wanted to."

Craig was very into athletics, especially baseball and football. Academics always took a backseat to infield practice or playing catch. In sixth grade Craig remembers a turning point of sorts when he performed in his first school play.

"I never got great grades. I remember when they had the tryouts I was shocked I got the lead role. I was always a disrupter, always wanted to make everybody laugh," Craig explains. "They had us read for these things and I got the lead part and I remember thinking, 'I'm good at something? This teacher is choosing me?' It was an easy thing for me to do. I don't remember the name of the play, but I remember it was about going to space."

Craig was excited that he had found an activity he could do besides sports. More important, it was something people admired and found somewhat intellectual.

Later on, as a student at York Suburban High School, Craig further honed his acting skills in the drama club. One of the school's most outstanding young actors, Craig traveled to a local acting competition and won first place. It was yet another turning point for him.

"I kind of made up my mind right then and there that if I didn't make it in sports I would do acting," Craig says, noting that he couldn't have done it without his family behind him.

"My parents came to every single event that I ever did in my life. They were so supportive of anything I did," Craig says.

After graduating from high school, Craig went on to play football at East Stroudsburg State University in East Stroudsburg, Pennsylvania. Craig was at college for two years before he dropped out to pursue an acting career.

"I blew my knee out and I really didn't go to class much," Craig says.

He decided that acting was really what he wanted to do, and nearby New York City was the perfect place to pursue a career. Craig was motivated to learn more about the craft that came so naturally to him. He announced his plans to the family and was surprised, pleasantly, at their response. He especially credits his mother, Anna, for standing behind him.

"From the day I wanted to go to New York, my mom completely supported what I wanted to do," Craig says. "She never missed one single play or anything I ever did."

Craig soon found work in the New York theater. In the early 1980s, actor Matthew Broderick had finished his run in the hit Broadway play *Torch Song Trilogy*; Craig took over the role of Alan.

Three years after Craig moved, his brother, Hogan, followed. Craig laughs when he thinks back to those early years in each of their careers. "We had an apartment with five other roommates, so we basically shared a double bed for two years," Craig says.

Hogan went on to develop a very successful writing career. He has won three Daytime Emmy Awards in the past few years for his work as a writer on the soap opera *As the World Turns*.

Speaking of soap operas, Craig's first television role was on the daytime drama *One Life to Live* in 1983. He played the love interest to a then-unknown actress, Faith Ford. He continued to pursue theater, television, and film work, eventually landing his breakthrough role in the romantic teen comedy *Some Kind of Wonderful*. The 1987 film, which also starred up-and-comers Eric Stoltz, Mary Stuart Masterson, and Lea Thompson, received great buzz and put Craig's name on Hollywood's short list of rising young talents.

Craig continued to land solid supporting roles in films and television for the next several years. Then, in 1992, he and another young actor named Brad Pitt starred as brothers in the Robert Redford–directed classic *A River Runs Through It*. The movie received massive critical acclaim and solidified Craig's status as a viable movie star. It did wonders for Brad Pitt, too.

Craig's list of credits throughout the 1990s boasts a wide variety of film projects (*Fire in the Sky, The Program, Sleep with Me*) and television roles (*In Pursuit of Honor, A Season in Purgatory, Miss Evers' Boys*).

When *One Tree Hill* came about, Craig found the underlying complexity of the characters' personal lives too intriguing to pass up. The small-town feel of the setting rekindles fond memories of his hometown of York, which Craig visits as often as he can.

"I always try to help young people out and give them a little direction," says Craig, who is often asked by kids from his alma mater how he went from being a small-town boy to a successful actor.

"I think it's real easy to look at what's out there and get discouraged. I was never the best-looking guy, I was never the Tom Cruise–looking guy. I think the biggest thing I can say is don't compare yourself. Focus on making you the best *you* you can be as an actor and follow your own path. You can't compare an apple to an orange. It will cause a lot of self-esteem issues."

Craig was confident he was making the right choice by accepting the *OTH* role. But there was a downside. As was the case for some of the other actors, Craig wasn't exactly thrilled to have to move away from his Los Angeles–area home.

"The people in Wilmington are great, but I've got this amazing home near a lake in the mountains and I miss it when I'm away," Craig says, noting that he comes back as often as he can to spend time with his daughter, Willow.

"I will come back whenever I have off three days in a row. I have it good because sometimes my scenes can all be shot in two days and then I won't work for the next four days. I'm lucky with days off and making all the family stuff work."

In his free time, Craig can usually be found reading or writing scripts, composing poetry, or working on his first novel, which he describes as a family drama.

"I intended to finish it last year, but I got caught up in this movie I was doing and I had no time to do anything else," Craig says, noting that he is "a two-hour- to three-hour-a-day writer. It's not discipline—I'm the most undisciplined person I know, but I just love to do it. If I had to force myself to do it I couldn't."

The movie that sidetracked Craig from working on his novel was one he had wanted to do for several years. He began writing his ideas down, which over the course of several years evolved into a full-length feature script he titled *American Crude*. Craig's vision became a reality with the film, which he says combines the elements of *Pulp Fiction, Blue Velvet,* and *After Hours.*

"It's its own little world," Craig says. "It's very dark humor."

Right before *OTH* shut down production for the Christmas holidays in December 2003, Craig decided he was going to go for it. He'd had the script written, and planned to produce and direct it, too. Making a movie is an expensive process and Craig had to come up with the funds to finance the project. He and his producing partner, Brad Kramer, began meeting with other producers and agents in Hollywood and soon they were able to raise some financing and attract very talented actors like Rob Schneider, Michael Clarke Duncan, and Jennifer Esposito.

Right after the first season of *OTH* ended, Craig was busy at work in Los Angeles filming *American Crude*. He worked day and night, right up until the time he had to return to Wilmington for the start of season two. Craig was able to keep the budget under $1 million, which is a very rare feat for a filmmaker to accomplish. He plans to release the movie in 2005.

In his free time, Craig enjoys photography, writing, and being outdoors. Even though he's been in the business for a very long time, he stays as far away from Hollywood as he can.

"Certain places have certain types of energy. I literally get panic attacks when I go to Hollywood if I'm not in and out of there. The energy there just doesn't fit my soul," Craig says.

Wilmington and *One Tree Hill*, however, are a perfect fit for Craig.

"It's a nonstress situation. Everybody wants the best for everybody," Craig says. "More than any film I've worked on, it's creatively really comfortable and collaborative. I couldn't be happier."

CHAPTER ELEVEN

Paul Johansson
Is Dan Scott

Dan Scott is a man who had a bright future when he was a teenager growing up in Tree Hill, North Carolina. As an outstanding basketball player, Dan was a symbol of hopes and dreams for the small town. He had a chance to go places and make a name for himself. But during his senior year he got Karen, his high school sweetheart, pregnant. Dan chose to follow his dreams of playing college basketball and abandoned Karen, who went ahead and had a son, Lucas.

While in college, Dan met Deb and she became pregnant with a son, Nathan. Dan married Deb, and together with their son they moved back to Tree Hill, where Dan built a successful business and bought expensive homes and great cars.

Like many people, Dan's reality differs from the smiling facade he displays in public. Dan resents having to abandon his athletic dreams to raise a family and as such, he pushes his son to pursue goals he himself couldn't attain.

Dan's controlling actions have a negative ripple effect on Nathan, Deb, his brother, Keith, and Karen and Lucas. But he doesn't see where he has gone wrong. Instead he blames and belittles others, all the while conniving to get his way.

"You can't have *Dallas* without J.R.," Paul says. "And this character believes he is right. He believes if you don't raise your kids to be strong, tough, and independent, you've failed as a parent. That's Dan's point of view. I couldn't imagine any other character I'd want to play."

Paul Johansson was born on January 26, 1964, in Spokane, Washington. He is the son of professional hockey player Earl "Ching" Johnson (a member of the 1954 Stanley Cup–winning Detroit Redwings team). Earl went by Johnson when he was playing hockey, but he later chose to change the family name to Johansson to reflect his Swedish heritage. When Paul was very young, his family moved from Washington State to nearby British Columbia, in Canada.

Because of his father's profession, young Paul took a liking to sports at an early age. He excelled at many sports, including hockey and basketball. Paul enjoyed the competitive nature and athletic skill both sports required. By the time he was in high school, Paul was a strapping six foot two and basketball had become his sport of choice.

Paul was also an excellent student. He was particularly fond of reading and loved daydreaming about the characters and their adventures.

"I was just very much of a reading kid. I read so much, a lot of my mentors were characters in books," Paul says. "I remember *A Farewell to Arms* and *The Sun Also Rises*. I always wanted to be someone other than who I was."

Paul became a star player for the Kelowna High School Owls basketball team, leading them to victory in the 1982 British Columbia high school championship game.

After graduating high school, Paul packed his bags for the University of British Columbia in Vancouver. He was there on a basketball scholarship and Paul applied himself as a student and an athlete. As the guard for the school team, the Thunderbirds, Paul was an all-star player. He regularly landed on the local paper's sports pages for his excellent—and at times aggressive—play.

While a student at UBC, Paul majored in English literature. He also discovered that acting was a great way to make a little cash and cover his university tuition bills. Paul was considered a rare commodity when he was in college. He was not only a stellar athlete but he had brains *and* good looks. Vancouver commercial agents quickly signed him up to appear in local ads for the British Columbia

Lottery and Budget Brake and Muffler, and national spots for Labatt's Lite beer.

The work was at times tedious. In the British Columbia Lottery ad, Paul plays a guy who walks into a store and purchases a lottery ticket from a pretty salesgirl who writes down her number and "Call Me" on the ticket. The guy then exits the store, gets into his pickup truck, and throws his cowboy hat out the window.

"It's a lot of hard work and very time-consuming," Paul says of commercial work. "We worked for twelve hours on the Lotto commercial and did fifty-one takes of just throwing the hat out of the truck window."

The money Paul earned from his acting gigs helped cover his $7,000-a-year tuition and expenses. At the time, Paul considered the acting a means to an end. He never thought of it as a possible career. Basketball was always at the top of his list.

In 1987 Paul was named to the All-Canadian basketball team. The distinction allowed Paul to play for his country and possibly make the Olympic team. It was a lifelong dream of Paul's to represent his country in the world's most prestigious sporting competition one day. He traveled around the world and received numerous offers to play professionally in the European league. But something Paul couldn't quite put his finger on had changed. He loved competing and he loved that he was so close to fulfilling his athletic dreams. But the more he thought about it, the more he knew that he had reached a fork in the road. Perhaps, he felt, basketball was something he could do for fun, while acting and entertainment could be more fulfilling over the long haul. After much agonizing, Paul said good-bye to basketball and instead decided to pursue acting.

It was a decision that didn't sit well with his father. Mr. Johansson was hoping his son would follow in his footsteps and have a successful athletic career. But he knew that it wasn't in Paul's heart. He respected his son's decision and wished him well.

"I didn't pursue acting," Paul explains. "It found me. Once I decided to do it, I made it a priority."

A good friend of Paul's was also an avid athlete-turned-actor. Like Paul, this young man—Jason Priestley—was making a name for himself in Vancouver acting circles. Jason was a young, rising talent, and he was encouraged by many casting directors and agents in Vancouver to head to Los Angeles, where he could be exposed to the entertainment business on a much grander scale.

Meanwhile, Paul had earned his bachelor's degree in English literature, and he was also considering a career in writing. Jason told Paul that he was planning to move to Los Angeles and asked if he wanted to come along. Paul figured that would be a great place to pursue both his dreams. So the two friends packed their bags and headed down the West Coast to Los Angeles. Armed with their talent and their dreams, the duo just knew great things lay ahead.

Sure enough, within no time Jason and Paul were landing acting work. Jason went on to star as Brandon Walsh on the massively popular TV show *Beverly Hills, 90210*. Paul, meanwhile, landed a starring role as Greg Hughes on the hit soap opera *Santa Barbara*. But Paul didn't lose his passion for writing. He knew that acting could be a great day job, so to speak, while he could focus on writing at night and on weekends. It was a win-win situation for Paul.

After a year on *Santa Barbara*, Paul's role was cut. On soap operas, characters often come and go in rapid-fire succession. Paul was bummed that he wasn't given a reason other than that his contract was up.

"They didn't even bother to write me out," Paul explains. "I don't get run over by a car or anything. I say, 'I'm tired. I think I'll go upstairs and take a nap.'"

Paul's soap opera character may have taken a long snooze, but his career was alive and kicking. Soon after he left *Santa Barbara*, Paul was cast in the feature film *Soapdish*. The movie was a spoof on today's soap operas and Paul was cast as the young, hunky husband to Sally Field's character, an aging soap star. The film received great reviews and Paul's performance didn't go unnoticed. He soon found himself back on television in the series *Parker Lewis Can't Lose*. The show focused on a teenage boy named Parker Lewis and his friends. Parker was a kind of cool, pop-culture-hip fellow. Paul played high school kid Nick Comstock. His run ended after two seasons when the show, despite great critical reviews, just didn't have enough of a mass following to stay on the air.

The timing was right for Paul to shift his focus back to writing. He decided to pack up his car and, once and for all, concentrate on writing a novel and seeing the country. A couple of weeks after leaving Los Angeles for wherever the road might take him, Paul received a phone call from his agent. The agent told Paul that producer Aaron Spelling wanted to see if he would audition for a role on *Beverly Hills, 90210*. Paul chuckled as he thought of his buddy Jason, who was *90210*'s big star. He thought it would be great if the two of them could work together.

"So I came back, and that was a big turnaround for me," says Paul, who landed the role of John Sears, a hunky, conceited fraternity boy who was interested in dating Kelly, *90210*'s blond bombshell played by actress Jennie Garth. John Sears was not the most upstanding guy on campus, which thrilled Paul to death.

"That role really broke me out in people's minds," Paul says. "I didn't have to play a goody-goody. I got to play somebody with an edge, which has been my forte ever since."

Paul's recurring role on *90210* gave him so much exposure, he was literally sifting through offers to appear in movie and television projects. His next notable project was the critically acclaimed television series *Lonesome Dove: The Outlaw Years.* Paul played Austin Peale, an alcoholic sheriff who is at odds with one of the town's central figures, a man by the name of Newt Call (played by actor Scott Bairstow).

Paul's career was sailing along when he was offered a national commercial for Diet Coke. The commercial featured Paul as a deliveryman carrying a case of the sodas into an office full of female secretaries. He opens one of the cans and chugs it while all of the women, their mouths agape, unabashedly stare. When he puts the can down, he smiles and walks away. A drop of soda rolls down the side of the can. One of the women makes a beeline for the can and catches the last drop between her lips. The 60-second commercial was a huge success and had everyone talking. Paul couldn't believe it.

"I was chopping carrots and saw the ad and went, 'Wow, that's me.' And then the phone rang until four A.M.," Paul says.

In 1998 Paul found himself offered yet another great role as Nick Wolfe in the series *Highlander: The Raven.* The show had a cult following and Paul developed quite a legion of loyal fans.

At about that same time, Paul reached a personal milestone when he wrote and directed his first short film, *Conversations in Limbo*. He based the movie on the Oscar Wilde short story "Day of Judgment." Paul financed the project and was able to count on friends like Jason Priestley, Nick Cassavettes, and Costas Mandylor to fill out the cast. The movie premiered at the 1999 Toronto Film Festival and is often screened on the Sundance Cable Channel.

Paul's writing aspirations continued to soar, and in 2003 he finished writing, directing, and producing *The Incredible Mrs. Ritchie*. The story is about a troubled teen who is given a second chance to repay his criminal debt to society. The movie stars Gena Rowlands and James Caan and aired on Showtime.

While writing is Paul's passion, acting opportunities too rich to turn down keep knocking on his door. He's spent the past ten years trying to finish that novel he set out to write back in the mid-1990s. But Paul has resigned himself to the fact that the novel will get finished in due time. When a good role comes along, he can't help but grab it.

In 2003 Paul was offered the role of Dan Scott in *One Tree Hill* and he just couldn't refuse. Paul could relate to Dan's love of basketball and his ambition. After all, he grew up the big basketball star in his hometown. But what really attracted Paul to the role more than anything was Dan's need for control and power.

"I think what's interesting about Dan Scott as a character is that he is dangerous," Paul says. "When the show is over you will remember Dan Scott."

Playing a thirty-something father on *One Tree Hill* is great fun for Paul. He enjoys the dichotomy of the town golden boy who seemingly has it all. But deep down, Dan has regrets about his own choices and takes it out on those who are close to him—mainly his son, Nathan; his brother, Keith; and his wife, Deb.

Dan Scott may be an unsavory character, but Paul is not. When he's not spending his free time reading, writing, traveling, or working out (he still picks up a basketball every now and again), Paul enjoys socializing with the cast and crew. Like Hilarie, Sophia, and Bethany Joy, Paul helps keep Wilmington's Port City Java in business by being a loyal customer.

"I love aging as an actor," Paul says. "So many doors are open to me now, so many character options. The thirties and forties are the best. You have a different mentality, too. There's an impending sort of, 'I'm truly in the middle of my existence.' In your twenties, you still think you're a sprout starting out."

Paul is having the time of his life and he looks forward to continuing to build a well-rounded career. "Anything that makes me better, that challenges me—a great role as an actor or something that I've written that I am so proud of," Paul says. "My best days are ahead of me."

CHAPTER TWELVE

Barry Corbin Is Coach Whitey Durham

Coach Whitey Durham is why Tree Hill has such a love affair with basketball. The 35-year veteran is a tough-as-nails, competitive-until-the-end type of guy. He convinced Dan Scott, a one-time promising player of his, to forget about his pregnant high school sweetheart and instead accept a college scholarship in hopes of someday making it to the big leagues. Now, sixteen years later, Whitey is confronted by the residual effects of his advice. He's now coaching Lucas and Nathan, Dan's two sons, who are both very talented players, yet grew up very differently. Lucas, after all, was never acknowledged by Dan. Until now.

Grizzly and stoic on the outside, Whitey is a teddy bear on the inside. He cares very much about his players, despite his strict coaching style. And he cares very much about fulfilling the promise he made to his wife decades earlier when he committed to coaching ball in Tree Hill.

Barry Corbin, the veteran stage, film, and television actor who plays Whitey, says the role of the coach jumped out at him the moment he read the script.

"When I read the pilot, it seemed to me it was a moral show, which is an odd thing to see these days," Barry says. "I felt that the coach was kind of the moral balance in the show."

It wasn't lost on Barry that *OTH* was generating buzz in Hollywood for being one of The WB's best new dramas.

"Also, it doesn't hurt for an older man like me to be seen by young people on a show every week. You've got to be a little careful when you're picking a part on a series. If it's a hit, you're stuck there. And so if I'm going to be stuck somewhere for seven years, I want it to be something I enjoy doing."

Acting wasn't a profession that ran in the Corbin family. Barry was born Leonard Barrie Corbin on October 16, 1940, to Kilmer Blain Corbin, an attorney, and Alma Corbin, an elementary school teacher in Lamesa, Texas.

Barry made his performing debut when he was six years old and sang at a Sunday church service. He loved performing and spent much of his time writing little neighborhood plays, playing guitar, or drawing cartoons. Most Saturdays Barry spent watching old westerns at the Majestic Theater in Lamesa.

Barry dreamed of playing a cowboy someday on the stage or the big screen. In high school, he appeared in school plays and musicals and later majored in theater at Texas Tech University.

At 21, Barry left college to join the Marine Corps and was stationed for two years at Camp Pendleton in Oceanside, California, the same base where *American Idol* singer Josh Gracin was stationed during his tour of duty.

Upon his honorable discharge, Barry returned to Texas and began to focus on a career in acting. He worked at numerous small theaters and festivals before ultimately relocating to New York. For the next decade and a half, Barry lived a vagabond actor's life, performing in regional theater and traveling from town to town. In 1979 he landed his big break with a supporting role in *Urban Cowboy*. The movie starred John Travolta and Debra Winger and was a huge hit. Soon after, roles followed in films like *Any Which Way You Can* and *Stir Crazy*.

Television also called upon Barry's talents. He landed major supporting roles in series such as *Dallas, Lonesome Dove*, and *Northern Exposure* (which garnered him two Emmy nominations for outstanding supporting actor during its run).

Since then, Barry has continued to star in film, television, and stage. Barry says each medium is special, but the stage is really where an actor can shine. "I think I like the stage because you have a direct interaction with the audience," Barry explains. "I do a one-man play where I interact with the audience, and that's always fun because it's always fresh. The audience is another character. The play is about a cattleman named Charlie Goodnight. He lived to be 96 years old and I play him at 96, just before Christmas. It's the night he died and he's sitting in his room talking about his life. He treats the audience as if they're intruders in his house. He starts out by really browbeating them, then he calms down and starts reminiscing. I've done it in Nevada, Texas, New Mexico. I'd love to do it in the East someday."

Barry has been on literally thousands of auditions in his career. So when he read for the role of Coach Whitey Durham, he knew he could play it one of two ways.

"I've got alopecia, which is when your immune system attacks your hair follicles. Nobody knows why it happens or what triggers it. It doesn't bother me at all, but I've got big gaps of baldness on my head," Barry explains. "I was wearing a wig when I auditioned for them and I said, 'Well, you've got me this way,' and then I pulled the wig off and I said, 'Or you've got me this way.' And they liked the bald look."

Barry was a natural for the role, even though he didn't know anything about basketball. But that's why it's called acting, Barry maintains. "I don't have to know what I'm doing, I just have to look like I know what I'm doing. I've played jet pilots, too, and I don't know squat about that, either."

Professional NBA players like Shaquille O'Neal and Michael Jordan are household names to sports lovers. But not for Barry, who really couldn't care less about the finesse of a three-point jump shot or the sheer power of a slam dunk. "I had never watched a basketball game until I got the part," Barry says, chuckling. "If I had to shoot a basketball it would be apparent that I don't know a thing about it."

Throughout his career Barry has played numerous tough guys, including military officers, cowboys, and sheriffs. At one point Barry says he put a moratorium on playing any character whose name began with Sheriff.

"Some actors specialize in playing lawyers or doctors," Barry explains. "I was always playing the sheriff role. So I turned down parts with 'Sheriff' for a year, and I turned down some pretty good parts. But after about a year they started coming around with some other roles. I've played sheriffs since then, but I think you've got to play as wide a variety of roles as you can possibly do."

Maintaining other interests is also key, Barry says. When he's not working, Barry can usually be found at the 15-acre ranch in Fort Worth, Texas, he shares with his daughter, Shannon Ross.

"I've got four head of cattle, seven miniature horses, three saddle horses. My daughter raises mastiff dogs, so we've got these big dogs in the yard," he says.

Summer days at the ranch are spent doing chores, feeding the animals, maintaining the grounds, and trying to stay cool. Barry rides every chance he gets—whether at work or play. In June 2004 he finished shooting *Molding Clay*, an independent film in which he rode horses.

Barry used to compete as a cutting horse rider and still attends rodeos and competitions such as the NCHA Summer Cutting Spectacular that takes place annually at the Will Rogers Memorial Coliseum in Fort Worth.

Because of his impressive body of work, Barry is often asked for advice by aspiring performers. His philosophy, which he applies to his daily life, is to keep things simple. "My advice when people ask me if they should pursue acting or the theater or movies or whatever as a career is think long and hard about it and think if there's anything else that can make you almost that happy," Barry explains. "If you can come up with anything, then don't do acting, because most people are not capable of facing the rejection actors face every day. You get it constantly and people say it's not personal. Well, the only thing we've got to sell is ourselves. So no matter how many times people say it's not personal, it is. It's very personal. Most people can't stand that kind of rejection and they go into a deep depression and leave the business."

Barry continues, "An example is, if you're in any other line of work, you maybe apply for ten jobs in a lifetime.

Maybe out of those ten you might be rejected five times. Actors are rejected five times before lunch. Also, it's a very competitive field. Acting is one of those things that everybody thinks they can do until they get up on a stage or get in front of a camera. We have to learn to play our bodies, our voices, our persona. We have to invent ourselves."

Acting by day and cowboying on the weekends, Barry says he's got the life he's always dreamed of. "I wouldn't trade places with anybody. I've been very lucky in the things I've been offered. Acting to me is this—a good part played well is like a good plumber putting in a bathroom. It requires some skill, it requires some technique, it requires some imagination, but really essentially what we're doing is telling a story. That's what actors are, storytellers."

CHAPTER THIRTEEN

Wilmington, North Carolina

Location, Location, Location

One of the first things people ask *One Tree Hill* creator Mark Schwahn is why does the show film in Wilmington, North Carolina? The answer is, simply put, why not?

While it might seem more ideal for the show to shoot in Los Angeles—the production company, the network, and the writing staff are based there—it is a luxury for the show to be able to shoot entirely on location. Sure, Tree Hill is a fictional town, but it's based in North Carolina. Wilmington, one of the largest seaports on the East Coast, doubles as Tree Hill with minimal effort. Its sandy beaches, historical architecture, and seasonal climate creates the perfect backdrop for the show.

"It feels like a small town and yet it's very expansive," Mark explains. "There's so many different tonal qualities to Wilmington. To be able to capture all types of textures and styles in one place and still make it feel specific and make it feel like you're in Tree Hill is wonderful."

Wilmington is the kind of town that has something for just about everyone. Located several miles inland, Wilmington is just a short drive from some of the best beaches in the country. The town is also home to the University of North Carolina at Wilmington campus and, as such, there's lots of youthful energy. Dance, theater, and music productions enjoy making a stop at Wilmington's historic Thalian Hall. Local artisans, jewelers, and potters sell their wares at craft shows and in small downtown shops and galleries.

For the outdoor enthusiast, there's plenty of boating, fishing, hiking, and mountain biking to be done at Wrightsville Beach, Kure Beach, Carolina Beach, or just about anywhere in and around the Cape Fear River.

History buffs can take a riverboat ride, explore the city's landmark architecture, and visit one of several museums in town.

Recently it's been a Hollywood trend to take a movie or television production to Canada. Vancouver has become an especially popular location over the years for shows like *The X-Files, Dark Angel,* and *Smallville.* There's a variety of reasons why shows go out of town. First of all, it's actually less expensive to have a production relocate out of the country than it is for the show to shoot in town.

Second, and maybe more important, there just aren't enough studios and soundstages in Los Angeles for each and every production to shoot. Luckily, the folks at *One Tree Hill* were able to land in Wilmington.

"We looked at some other locations, but as soon as we got here we could feel it," Mark explains. "There's a really good energy here."

The producers of *Dawson's Creek* felt the same way when they chose Wilmington as a home base from 1998 to 2003. However, *Dawson's Creek* was set on Cape Cod, in Massachusetts, which meant a lot of the city couldn't be showcased because it would be a dead giveaway to the viewer that it wasn't really the Cape. The *One Tree Hill* gang can be a bit more liberal with their choices because the show takes place in a southeastern North Carolina town.

"Wilmington is not a huge town, so it's not like we can go with a completely different look," producer Greg Prange explains. "But we've tried to make it a different show and have not tried to imitate what we did on *Dawson's Creek.*"

Still, Greg says, the town does have a special flavor that the show strives to capture. "We try to make the town a character," Greg says. "We're not calling it the smallest town in the world, but we're not calling it a major metropolitan city. We like to show a little bit of the plainness and at the same time show that we're in the twenty-first century. Everybody has their BlackBerrys and cell phones and all that stuff."

When the script calls for shooting indoors—like a scene in Lucas's or Nathan's bedrooms, then the production sets up shop at Screen Gems Studios. Screen Gems is the biggest film and television production lot on the East Coast. Nine soundstages sit on the 32-acre lot where more than 300 productions (including *Dawson's Creek, Divine Secrets of the Ya-Ya Sisterhood, Domestic Disturbance, Weekend at Bernie's,* and *A Walk to Remember*) have been shot. The *One Tree Hill* set can be seen up close on the one-hour Screen Gems Studio tour.

Generally, when a television show needs to film a scene on public property—a park or a city street—the production must obtain a permit. In bigger towns like Los Angeles and New York, obtaining a permit can be a bit of an exhausting process.

"In a lot of cities, especially Los Angeles, it's all about permits and controlling traffic and things of that nature," Mark explains. "I think Wilmington is more amenable to the filmmaking process because they've seen it with *Dawson's,* so it's a luxury to be able to go into real neighborhoods and not have it be a huge thing that really slows down the company."

It's big business putting together a television show, and the folks in Wilmington know it. In addition to boasting top-notch facilities, Wilmington's production crews and actors are more than capable. Some of the team that works on *One Tree Hill* is from Los Angeles, but many of the staff hail from Wilmington and have worked on Wilmington-based film and television projects for years. Many local actors work as extras on the various productions throughout the year.

"We shot a lot of basketball in the first season so we had to fill the gym quite a bit," Mark explains. "All of the extras were local hires from the Wilmington area. The kids on the Ravens basketball team—with the exception of about three actors—were all actors from the Wilmington area."

Wilmington has embraced the show and made the entire cast and production crew feel extremely welcome.

"Everyone here is so wonderful," Sophia says. "People are warm and inviting. You can stop in a store and end up chatting with the owner for an hour, sharing an iced tea. It's incredible, and it's great, too, because no one here cares about the show too much. There's none of that celebrity nonsense. No one treats us differently. We lead normal lives. It's awesome!"

Home Sweet Home

Wilmington isn't just a home away from home for the *One Tree Hill* cast and crew. Many members of the production are from Los Angeles or New York and had to leave their city lives in order to work on the show. Though they might have been sad about having to relocate, Greg Prange says practically all of them are ecstatic about their new digs.

"It's a really nice place to live," Greg says simply. "Being out of Los Angeles, there's a little bit of the reality that you're not quite in the Hollywood flow. So in some ways work becomes a bit more of a priority because that's what we're here for. I think in some ways it helps the young talent focus better. There's not quite so many outside distractions. I think for the overall creativity of the show and their dedication to it, I think in a strange way it kind of helps. We're much more of a family. We all hang together more."

"They call it the blackhole because once you come here you never want to leave," Hilarie says. "I never thought I would love any place more than I love New York. It's a huge part of my soul. But this is such a beautiful, lively place. When I was little, we came here on family vacations. It was weird because for the first couple of months I felt like I was on vacation. But then I got to noticing how perfect it was here."

"Wilmington is inland and it's like an old Southern town," Craig says. "It's got a lot of character. It's a great place to spend a week or two. The people are really nice, like no place else. There's a lot of cool stuff to do, gardens and plantations. The city is right on Cape Fear River and there's a lot of old buildings and cotton mills. There's just an energy that's conducive to writing and I find I write like crazy down there."

Bethany Joy says she, too, is creatively inspired when she's in Wilmington. "During Hurricane Charlie I just sat in my apartment, looked out the window and watched the rain, and thought, Wow . . . this is beautiful. I just wrote and wrote and it was the greatest feeling. I love it here. I can see why so many artists live here."

"It's not very typical, you know. When you go off to film a TV show you're usually in Hollywood or Burbank, but they definitely have a good infrastructure for film in Wilmington," James says. "When you're on set it's a whole heck of a lot different. The setting is beautiful and the community is great."

And when the cast and crew aren't working, the city is a nice place to be, too. Hilarie, Bethany, and Sophia have combed practically every inch of Wilmington and happily give it a thumbs-up.

"I tend to spend my time either walking around downtown, stopping in my favorite shops and antique stores with my friends, having lunch at Café Phoenix, or hanging out at home with Chad and the dogs," Sophia says. "We go to the movies, to the beach when it's warm. The boys have their football games on Saturday afternoons. Oliver Beanie and Cecil and Edge of Urge are my favorite stops for shopping."

"You drive down Main Street and there's Spanish moss hanging from the trees and all the trees shadow the road. Every house is perfect. It's like these little dollhouses all over the place," Hilarie explains. "Then you go into town and you get coffee—and it's not Starbuck's coffee, it's Port City Java. This town has its own coffee empire! Everyone is so friendly. It's a college town. So everyone is young. You're ten minutes away from the beach, the art scene is amazing. It's a perfect mix of the old historic—with the architecture and tradition—and the young, with the college area and the beach.

"I'm so inspired here. I've never had so much creative energy. It's hard to be inspired when you're living in a closet in New York. Down here I sit in my old house and I have the windows open and I can hear the trolley go by, the horse and carriage go by. It's a really friendly neighborhood. It's a very warm atmosphere. I think I would still love it even if I didn't have New York to compare it to. I'm madly in love with both places."

CHAPTER FOURTEEN

Behind the Scenes at *One Tree Hill*

Visiting the set of *One Tree Hill* requires a car, a map, and a lot of time. That's because the show is filmed on many sets located in and around Wilmington, North Carolina.

The main location for the show is at the Screen Gems studio lot. Screen Gems houses sets for all of the teen characters' bedrooms because, as creator Mark Schwahn explains, "We spend a lot of time in their bedrooms. When I was in high school that's where I spent a lot of my time. It's your safe haven, so those are all on set."

Karen's Cafe is located in an abandoned storefront on Front Street in downtown Wilmington. The production was able to secure a lease on the property and turn the location into a veritable soundstage with props, lights, and sound equipment. Unlike other soundstages, though, Karen's Cafe is used inside and outside. For example, when Haley sits down at the counter for a cup of coffee, the street-side window might be in the background. Usually when these types of scenes are done, the cars and trucks passing by are hired extras. But on this show the traffic you see is real. Indeed, actual Wilmington life is captured in the background shots.

The last part of the shooting puzzle is the character's respective homes and Tree Hill High School. The homes are located in various parts of town, depending on the character who lives there. For example, Nathan's house is located in a sprawling residential area while Lucas and Karen's place is closer to town. Dan's beach house is located about 15 miles from downtown in the popular vacation town of Carolina Beach.

A Day in the Life

The key to a good cast and crew is that they do some very hard work and all the while make it look fun and easy. Well, the fun part is a no-brainer with this gang. They have a genuine passion for what they do and, therefore, enjoy putting the show together. But the work is anything but easy. It takes many individuals and many hours in a given day to put together the one-hour drama.

A typical day on the set of *One Tree Hill* begins at about five A.M. The production crew—the folks who light the set and operate the cameras, plus the director and the hair, wardrobe, and makeup staff—are usually the first to arrive at work.

The actors who have a morning call time (usually six A.M.), arrive promptly so that their hair can be styled and their makeup can be applied in time for them to shoot their first scene. There's a saying that time is money, and that certainly is the case for those who work in television. Because so many people are needed to put the show together, it's crucial that everyone shows up on time and ready for work. Executive producer Greg Prange says that's never an issue at *One Tree Hill.*

"Everybody is prepared. That's the most important thing," Greg says. "The actors show up ready. They often have seven or eight pages of stuff to memorize for that day and they always know their lines."

While some actors need to be at work early, others are called in later in the day, depending on what type of scene is being shot.

"You can't really predict the schedule because you never know when you're going to be working," James says. "Things change, the scripts change, and you just have to go with the flow."

"The part that gets really difficult is the nighttime scenes," Greg explains. "You know teenagers, they like to get out and get in trouble or have fun at night, so we depict that on the show. Sometimes when we get to the end of the workweek an actor's call time might not be until noon or one in the afternoon, but then we'll go until two or three in the morning. Unfortunately that tends to happen a lot."

The toughest scenes to shoot are the basketball games. The high school gym has to be filled with extras, actors whose job it is to be part of the crowd in the background at the gym. Extras usually don't have any lines at all. Instead, they act like a real crowd would at a basketball game. During the show's first season, many basketball scenes were shot because it was crucial to the storyline between Nathan, Lucas, and Dan. The cast and crew often had to work on Sundays because that was the only day that the Laney High School gym was available to them.

"The basketball scenes are difficult because we often have to be in the gym all day," creator Mark Schwahn explains. "It's hard to keep everyone's energy up. We often shoot with multiple cameras when we shoot those scenes—three and four cameras at once—because there are so many pieces to those action sequences. It has to be authentic. I've always thought of the basketball on our show as the equivalent of somebody else's car chase."

When an episode wraps, there's very little time for rest. The cast is already memorizing lines while the crew is prepping for the next week's shoot.

"The actors get very little time for turnaround," Mark says. "It's a full-time job for them. It's up to them while working on one episode and acting to begin preparing and memorizing the next episode. They are constantly in motion and they're all professionals."

Home Sweet Home

Each of the actors has a trailer with his or her character's name on the outside. Having trailers instead of dressing rooms is a must because the show films in many different locations from week to week. The actors can sometimes work up to sixteen hours in a given day and therefore need a private space that is constant and personal. Of course, the trailer isn't the property of the actor. It belongs to the studio. But because the cast spends so much time in their trailers, they have the freedom to make that space their own, kind of like a home away from home.

Chad's trailer not only allows him a place to rest but it's a place where he can keep up with what's happening in the football world. During the show's first season, the cast and crew often had to work on weekends to accommodate the network schedule. The intensive workweek put a pang in the pit of Chad's stomach because, like everybody else who works on the show, he was used to having Sundays off. Sundays, after all, were meant for snacks and sodas and football.

"Football is big with our group," Craig says. "Chad has

satellite in his trailer and we all go over there to watch the football games on Sundays because we're generally working on Sundays."

"Hilarie and I have joint trailers," Sophia explains. "I can always run over and hang out with her. To make my trailer homey I brought bedding in for my couch—it folds out for naptime. I have a comforter and throw pillows, plus some cool lamps for nicer lighting, desk organizers, and a nice space for my computer. I love to decorate, so my trailer was a mini-project."

Sophia definitely wins the prize for having the homiest trailer! The others also decorated their spaces with personal photographs, stereos, candles, and pillows. Oftentimes Bethany Joy can be found strumming on her guitar or sipping a hot mug of tea in her trailer, while Hilarie is most likely knitting, reading, or listening to music.

"It all depends on what we did the night before," Hilarie says. "In between scenes if we're doing something light-hearted, we hang out and talk and goof around. But if we worked late the night before we might want to take a break and be alone in our trailer or, if there's time, go home and take a nap."

Craig can often be found in his trailer reading or writing, while Moira is likely to make a quick phone call to talk to her husband and two kids.

James doesn't spend too much time in his trailer,

though he does have a PlayStation 2 machine at the ready for any willing challenger.

"I try to get some reading done. I have a little TV in there and I like to play video games with somebody else who has a little downtime," James says. "There's always something to do to pass the time. You can always read the next scene in the script. There's always work to do."

And there's always food to eat. In the industry, the on-set kitchen and food area is known as Craft Services. Meals are provided for the whole production throughout the day. Breakfast can be something as simple as a toasted bagel, or something more elaborate like an omelet and pancakes. Lunch and dinner are often salads, soups, sandwiches, pasta dishes, and grilled chicken or seafood.

Throughout the day the cast and crew can grab nutritious snacks like fruit, crackers and cheese, and water, or they can indulge in tasty treats like candy bars, chips, and sodas.

"They take good care of us," Hilarie says. "I'm not big on the healthy. I'm not that guy. I'm the girl that eats chocolate and drinks coffee and there's always plenty of that."

The Joke's On You

Every movie and television set has its pranksters, and *One Tree Hill* is no exception. The cast and crew get along extremely well, which makes for a pleasant work environment.

Periodically, Greg says, everyone on the set at one time or another has taken liberty to have a little fun.

"Probably Chad is the biggest prankster," Greg confesses. "He likes to keep things loose and as light as he possibly can. He likes to mess around and joke with people."

In between scenes it's rare for Chad not to engage in some kind of conversation with someone on the set. He's a genuine people person and is happy when those around him are having as much fun as he is at work. Chad is also the kind of person who manages to keep really quiet and poker-faced when he's pulling a prank.

During the show's first season, Chad slipped onto the set unnoticed and rearranged some magnets on the refrigerator door in Karen's house. After Chad's mastery, the once randomly placed magnets spelled out a not-for-publication type of sentence. Chad, who was just having fun, wanted to see if anyone would notice before he changed them back. But for a while, nobody did. The camera and lighting crews were hard at work setting up for the next scene and didn't notice the message on the refrigerator until the actors were just about to take their marks.

"Thank goodness it was caught and we were able to come off with the shot and change it," Greg says. "That prank was not such a good one."

More often than not the cast spends less time pulling pranks on one another and more time getting to know one another. Because the cast is together so much—both at work and during off-hours—they know one another's likes and dislikes. It's not unusual for Paul to meet Hilarie for coffee, or for Craig and Moira to grab dinner in town. Bethany Joy, Hilarie, and Sophia can often be found shopping at one of Wilmington's finest unique clothing stores, The Edge of Urge. Chad and James enjoy staying in shape and work out as regularly as possible. Barry is a horse enthusiast and has become well acquainted with Wilmington's rancher community. Moira enjoys spending time with her husband and kids on weekends.

Every so often, big groups that include the cast and members of the production staff get together and go to dinner in Wilmington. When the gang is together, there is never a lack of laughter and enthusiasm and storytelling.

"It's a very communal group, which is a big reason why I like going to work. It's a good group of people," Craig says. "Barry is phenomenally smart. He and I like to go out and have a couple of drinks. There's this one bar we go to and they have a Trivial Pursuit game on a screen and Barry never loses. It doesn't matter how many people come into that bar, the guy knows everything."

"Hilarie is constantly building something or knitting something or digging something," Bethany Joy says, laughing. "Sophia is the coordinator. She is always getting people together, making the phone calls, arranging the dinners, and making sure no one is excluded."

The feeling among the gang is downright familial, largely due to the fact that they are living in a small town, far away from many of Hollywood's distractions.

"We go out to dinner with each other, we go to the mall, we go to the grocery store, we watch movies at each other's houses and it's normal and it's great," Sophia says, noting that she diligently documents her life. "I run around with my little digital camera and take photos of people to put in my scrapbooks."

"We've been through a lot in two years and it's only brought us closer.

"We work together, we play together," Hilarie agrees. "You go into town on your days off and you see half the people you work with. It's a very nurturing atmosphere. There's a camaraderie that we have and I'm very proud of it."

Team Spirit

Socializing is one thing, but the *One Tree Hill* gang takes hanging out to a new level. Not only do they work together and break bread together but they also play together. On weekends it's a common sight to see many of the cast and crew clad in sweats at the local park playing touch football. Yes, football. Even though this is a show about basketball, the cast and crew (just in case it wasn't obvious) are nutty about football. Chad, *One Tree Hill*'s number one football fanatic, enlisted a majority of the cast and crew to play.

"We had six teams, about 35 to 40 people, some of the crew and their friends," Craig says. "Every Saturday we played and we had referees. It was a blast."

"It was a really big deal," Greg says. "At the end of the season we played a championship game and publicized it to the press. We raised money for the Pop Warner leagues here. They try to give a little bit back to the community and it's really good. A lot of young kids want to come and watch and it's something else. The guys and girls on this show have such great hearts."

Taking a cue from Chad's football venture, James helped organize a similar fund-raiser involving his favorite sport— basketball. With the support of the actors who play on the Tree Hill Ravens basketball team, James put together a charity basketball game. James and the Tree Hill Ravens played a team comprised of area high school all-stars. The result was phenomenal. More than three hundred people filed into the Laney High School gym that night, with the money raised earmarked for youth sports programs in the area. Bethany Joy kicked off the night by singing an incredible version of the national anthem. Then the game began. The guys hooped it up, all in the name of charity. Plenty of autographs were signed and pictures taken. In the end, it was agreed that the game was so successful—$5,000 was raised—it should become an annual event.

While the girls—Hilarie, Sophia, and Bethany Joy—don't play football or basketball, they don't just sit idly by. They are supportive of the guys in their own way. All three take on cheerleading duties when the guys play.

"I've cheered for football for nine years. I know what I'm doing," says Hilarie, a tomboy at heart who could probably hold her own on the field and the basketball court.

"I'm a football mom," Sophia says. "I make sure everybody is eating and staying hydrated."

"They're a really good-hearted bunch. They've got good heads on their shoulders," Greg says.

Barry, the most senior member of the cast, agrees.

"They're a delightful bunch of young people," Barry says proudly. "Not only are they good actors, they're good people. It's fun to watch them grow."

CHAPTER FIFTEEN

Fast Facts

CHAD MICHAEL MURRAY

FULL NAME: Chad Michael Murray

NICKNAME: Chad

BIRTH DATE: August 24, 1981

ASTROLOGICAL SIGN: Virgo

BIRTHPLACE: Buffalo, New York

CURRENT RESIDENCE: Los Angeles, California, and Wilmington, North Carolina

PARENT: Dad, Rex, is an air traffic controller.

SIBLINGS: Has three brothers (Rex, Brandon, Nick), one sister (Shannon), and one half brother (Tyler)

HAIR: Dirty blond

EYES: Blue

HEIGHT: 6'

PETS: A dog, Joe

HIGH SCHOOL: Clarence High School in Buffalo, NY (class of 1999)

BIG BREAK: Recurring role as prep student Tristan DuGrey on *Gilmore Girls*

<u>FAVORITES</u>
FOOD: Pepperoni pizza
BEVERAGE: Snapple
SPORT: Football
TEAM: Buffalo Bills
HOBBIES: Inline skating, soccer, volleyball, pickup basketball and football
ICE CREAM: Mint chocolate chip
CLOTHING: Blue jeans and a T-shirt
FASHION ACCESSORY: Wears a hemp necklace his father gave him
ACTORS: Robert DeNiro, Edward Norton, Al Pacino, Sean Penn
ACTRESSES: Natalie Portman
MUSIC: Incubus, Dave Matthews Band
MOVIES: *Fight Club*
TV: *The Simpsons*
BOOK: *The Catcher in the Rye*, by J.D. Salinger
PET PEEVE: Chad dislikes when people leave the cereal box open.
DATING RULE OF THUMB: "The woman is always right."
WHAT HE LIKES IN A GIRL: Someone who likes

to talk, intelligence, charm, a sweet disposition, and a good sense of humor
WHAT HE DISLIKES IN A GIRL: Party girls

HILARIE BURTON

FULL NAME: Hilarie Burton
NICKNAME: H-Bomb
BIRTH DATE: July 1, 1982
ASTROLOGICAL SIGN: Cancer
BIRTHPLACE: Sterling Park, Virginia
CURRENT RESIDENCE: New York and Wilmington, North Carolina
PARENTS: Father, Bill, an antique collector and mother, Lisa, a real estate agent
SIBLINGS: Three younger brothers—Billy (Billy Awesome), Johnny (Johnny Kickass), and Conrad (C-Rock)
HAIR: Brown with blond highlights
EYES: Green
HEIGHT: 5'8"
PETS: Poe, a cat (named after writer Edgar Allan Poe)
HIGH SCHOOL: Parkview High School in Sterling

Park, VA (Class of 2000)

COLLEGE: Fordham University at Lincoln Center and New York University (Hilarie is currently on a leave from college while she works on *TRL* and *One Tree Hill*.)

BIG BREAK: Landing a full-time VJ gig on MTV's *Total Request Live* in 2000

FAVORITES

FOOD: Dual-meat barbecuing—cook some chicken and some steak and share with your dinner mates. It's a tradition with Hilarie and her brother Billy.

HOBBIES: Collects antiques, knits and crochets

ICE CREAM: Chocolate

BEVERAGE: Coffee or grape-flavored Propel water

SNACK: Chocolate—especially Hershey's Nuggets. "They are curved on the top and it fits the roof of your mouth perfectly," Hilarie says.

CLOTHING: Cowboy boots—"a must!" Hilarie says. "They go on every trip with me."

FASHION: Vintage clothing. Hilarie often buys non-designer items she finds on what she calls "shopping treasure hunts."

STORE: Wal-Mart

BEAUTY PRODUCT: Dark mascara and blush

(She likes to experiment with different brands all the time.)

ACTORS: Bruce Campbell, William H. Macy

ACTRESSES: Angelina Jolie, Barbra Streisand, Ileana Douglas, Beth Grant

MUSIC: Loretta Lynn, Dolly Parton, Elvis Costello, David Bowie, and Elvis Presley

MOVIES: *Funny Lady* and *Coal Miner's Daughter*

TV: *Freaks and Geeks* (Hilarie travels with the DVD boxed set.)

HOLIDAY: Fourth of July. "My birthday is July first and my best friend's birthday is July fifth so it's always been a favorite holiday. It's all about having a cooler full of sodas, hot dogs, and just hanging out and shooting off firecrackers, being low-key, watching the fireworks. There's something about a holiday that isn't all about how much money you spend."

BOOK: *Dandelion Wine* by Ray Bradbury

AUTHORS: Ray Bradbury and F. Scott Fitzgerald

PET PEEVE: Guys who wear flip-flops with jeans or khakis. "If it's cold enough to wear pants, then wear real shoes. If it's warm enough to wear flip-flops, then wear shorts," Hilarie says. "It makes me crazy!"

WHAT SHE LIKES IN A PERSON: Loyalty

WHAT SHE DISLIKES IN A PERSON: Selfishness

ADVICE TO ASPIRIING PERFORMERS: "Go where the opportunity is. A lot of people want to act or sing or make music, but until you fully commit to it and go where the opportunity is, you're only putting half of your heart into it. You can get some experience acting wherever you are, but if you really want to pursue it you need to go to a bigger city like New York or Los Angeles."

JAMES LAFFERTY

FULL NAME: James Lafferty
BIRTH DATE: July 25, 1985
ASTROLOGICAL SIGN: Leo
BIRTHPLACE: Hemet, California
CURRENT RESIDENCE: Hemet and Wilmington, North Carolina
PARENTS: Mom, Angie; dad, Jeff
SIBLINGS: One brother, Stuart
HAIR: Brown
EYES: Blue
HEIGHT: 6'1"
PETS: A dog, Nino (a husky/shepherd mix)
HIGH SCHOOL: Hemet High School (Class of 2003)

COLLEGE: California State University at Long
Beach (James was enrolled until he landed his role
on *One Tree Hill*. He plans to return to school after
the show ends and major in international studies.)
BIG BREAK: *Emeril*—in 2001 James was cast as
the famous chef's son in his short-lived NBC sitcom.

<u>FAVORITES</u>
SPORT: Basketball
TEAM: Los Angeles Lakers
HOBBIES: Playing basketball, video games, going
to movies
ICE CREAM: Chocolate
SNACK: Fruit—peaches and oranges are James's
favorites
BEVERAGE: Root beer
ACTORS: Tom Hanks, Edward Norton
ACTRESSES: Natalie Portman, Rachel McAdams
MUSIC: Eminem, Gemini, Steve Miller Band, Geto
Boys
MOVIES: *Fight Club, Beautiful Girls*
TV: *The Sopranos, The Daily Show, South Park*
HOLIDAY: Fourth of July. "I always have the most
fun on the Fourth of July. You don't have to exchange
any gifts. You just go to the beach and watch fire-
works. It's always fun."

BOOKS: *The Iliad* by Homer
PET PEEVE: "When I'm trying to go to sleep and there are little noises, like a clock ticking or a fan squeaking, it drives me completely insane."
ADVICE TO ASPIRING PERFORMERS: "It's not an easy game. You've got to be a dreamer to do it, but you've also got to be willing to work hard. I always believed if you put the work in you'll get the benefits. This is an unstable business, also, so don't let that be the only thing you depend on. Make sure you have a fall-back. But most important, don't give up."

BETHANY JOY LENZ

FULL NAME: Bethany Joy Lenz
NICKNAME: Martha Stewart, Joiter
BIRTH DATE: April 2, 1981
BIRTHPLACE: Hollywood, Florida
HOME: Vancouver, Washington
HAIR: Brownish-blond
EYES: Brown
HEIGHT: 5'4"
PETS: Two cats, Noah and Allie
HIGH SCHOOL: Eastern Christian High School

(Class of 1999)
BIG BREAK: *Guiding Light*—a nine-episode stint
as teenage clone Reva Shayne

<u>FAVORITES</u>
FOOD: Hush puppies, lobster, warm bread, chicken
nuggets, and baby back ribs
SPORT: Rugby, hockey
HOBBIES: Writing, horseback riding, knitting, and
making stationery
DESSERT: Creme brulee and sticky rice with mango
BEVERAGE: Hot Earl Grey tea with honey and milk
ICE CREAM: Toasted coconut
ACTORS: John Cusack, Christian Bale, Johnny
Depp, Joseph Fiennes, and Joaquin Phoenix
ACTRESSES: Meryl Streep, Cate Blanchett, Liv
Tyler, and Tea Leoni
MUSIC: U2, Coldplay, and anything that's not a
sellout
MOVIES: *The Princess Bride, The Notebook,
Braveheart,* and *Equilibrium*
TV: *Joan of Arcadia, Alias, I Love Lucy, Lost,
Arrested Development*
HOLIDAY: Christmas. "It will always be number
one on my list. You feel cozy for like two months
straight. You sing songs, all the stores look exactly

the same. There's no other holiday where everybody decorates. There's a joy and a spirit of excitement that's in the air around Christmastime. It's the best."

BOOKS: The *Chronicles of Narnia,* by C. S. Lewis, and *Wild at Heart,* by John Eldredge

PET PEEVE: When people chew with their mouth open; when people say "ex-press-o"

WHAT SHE LIKES IN A PERSON: Vulnerability, compassion, humility

WHAT SHE DISLIKES IN A PERSON: Secrets, arrogance, and denial

ADVICE TO ASPIRING PERFORMERS: "You've got to have a passion for it and don't be easily discouraged. And don't approach it like, 'I have to get this job.' Go in and have fun. When I go out on auditions I look at it like I'm getting to play. I have a good time while I'm there and when it's over I forget about it."

SOPHIA BUSH

FULL NAME: Sophia Bush
NICKNAME: Soph
BIRTH DATE: July 8, 1982
ASTROLOGICAL SIGN: Cancer

BIRTHPLACE: Pasadena, California
CURRENT RESIDENCE: Pasadena and
Wilmington, North Carolina
PARENTS: George, a photographer, and Maureen, a
photography studio manager
HAIR: Brown
EYES: Brown
HEIGHT: 5'7"
PETS: Four dogs, one chameleon, one turtle
HIGH SCHOOL: Westridge School in Pasadena,
California (Class of 2000)
COLLEGE: University of Southern California
BIG BREAK: The feature film *Van Wilder* in 2002

<u>FAVORITES</u>
FOOD: Sushi, steak, and mashed potatoes
SPORT: Football
TEAM: USC Trojans
HOBBIES: Reading, photography, scrapbooking
SNACK: Chips and guacamole, macaroni and cheese
ICE CREAM: Chocolate chip cookie dough
DESIGNERS: Marc Jacobs, Donna Karan, Chloe, Ya-Ya
ACTORS: Sean Penn, Edward Norton, Robin
Williams
ACTRESSES: Meryl Streep, Nicole Kidman,
Charlize Theron

MUSIC: Josh Kelley, Maroon 5, Damien Rice,
N.E.R.D., Aerosmith

TV: *Law and Order*

DVD: "I own four copies of Robin Williams's *Live on Broadway* comedy special for HBO," Sophia says proudly. "One in Wilmington, one in L.A., one in my trailer, and one at my parents' house. I can watch it over and over again and it never gets old. He is the funniest, wittiest man on the planet!"

AUTHOR: Paul Coelho, Mitch Albom

PET PEEVE: People who leave their blinkers on after they've changed lanes

QUALITIES SHE LIKES IN A PERSON: Honesty, enthusiasm, intelligence, confidence

QUALITIES SHE DISLIKES IN A PERSON: Jealousy, dishonestly, false kindness. "I have walked away from friendships when I've realized that someone smiles to someone's face and talks about them the minute they walk out of a room. I have no room in my life for that kind of negative energy anymore," Sophia says.